Junior MasterChef

ULTIMATE RECIPE COLLECTION

ALYSHA

CHANDLER

HANNAH

DEE

CAROLINE

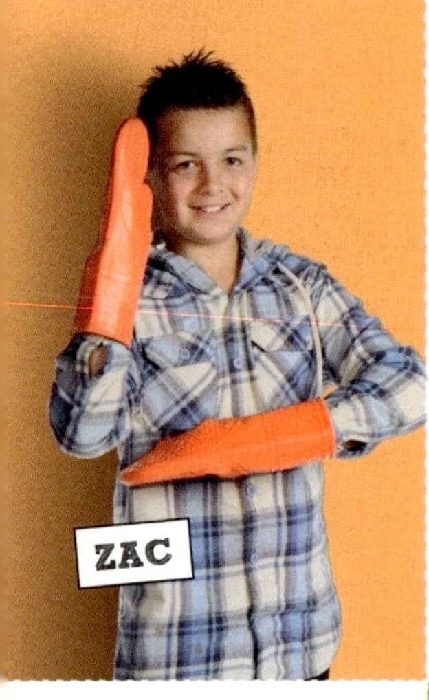
ZAC

MIRAEDE

MARCUS

MADI

JADE

GRETA

KIEREN

LILY

STEVEN

GRACIE

HARRY

AYA

TOM
JACK
INDIGO

CoNtenTs

about STApleS

Mayonnaise

MAKES: 2 CUPS
PREPARATION: 10 MINS

4 egg yolks
1 tbs lemon juice
Pinch of sea salt flakes
500ml (2 cups)
  vegetable oil

1 Making mayonnaise with a balloon whisk
Place a bowl on a folded damp tea towel (this will stop it slipping). Place egg yolks, lemon juice and salt in bowl and whisk until combined. Whisking continuously, gradually add oil, drop by drop at first, until mixture starts to thicken slightly. Add remaining oil in a thin, steady stream until it thickens and emulsifies. Season with salt and pepper.

2 Making mayonnaise with a food processor
Process egg yolks, lemon juice and salt in a food processor until combined. With the motor running, slowly add oil, drop by drop at first until mixture starts to thicken slightly. Add remaining oil in a thin, steady stream until mixture thickens and emulsifies. Season with salt and pepper. Transfer to an airtight container. Keeps refrigerated for up to 5 days.

To make aïoli (garlic mayonnaise), add 2 crushed cloves of garlic to 1 quantity of mayonnaise.

MIX IT UP

Tartare sauce
Place 1 quantity mayonnaise, 2 tbs diced pickled cucumber, 2 tbs chopped baby capers, 1 tbs chopped flat-leaf parsley, 1 tbs lemon juice and 1 tsp white vinegar in a bowl. Stir to combine. Season with salt and pepper. Makes 2 cups.

Caesar dressing
Place 1 quantity mayonnaise, 2 crushed cloves garlic, 4 anchovy fillets, 2 tsp Worcestershire sauce, 60ml (¼ cup) lemon juice and 100g grated parmesan in a food processor and process until smooth. Season with salt and pepper. Makes 3 cups.

Chicken caesar wrap
Place 2 slices white lavash bread on a chopping board and spread each with 1 tbs caesar dressing. Divide 2 cups shredded barbecue chicken, 6 baby cos leaves and 4 grilled rashers of bacon between bread slices. Roll up and serve immediately, or wrap rolls with baking paper and refrigerate until ready to serve. Makes 2.
MY SCORE   /10

Pesto pasta
Place 350g farfalle (bow-tie pasta) in a large
saucepan of boiling salted water and cook for
5 minutes or until pasta is al dente. Drain,
reserving 125ml (½ cup) cooking water. Place
pasta, ¾ cup pesto and reserved cooking water
in a bowl and toss well to combine. Divide among
bowls and serve scattered with roasted pine nuts,
basil leaves and shaved parmesan. Serves 4.

MY SCORE   /10

Pesto

MAKES: 1½ **CUPS**
PREPARATION: 10 MINS

1 cup (loosely packed)
   basil leaves
1 cup (loosely packed)
   flat-leaf parsley
100g pine nuts, roasted
2 cloves garlic, crushed
250ml (1 cup) olive oil
50g parmesan,
   finely grated

1 **Making the pesto**
Place basil, parsley, pine nuts and garlic in a food processor and process until combined. Add oil and process until smooth and combined. Transfer mixture to a bowl, add parmesan and stir to combine. Place pesto in an airtight container and cover surface closely with a sheet of baking paper before sealing with a lid. Keeps refrigerated for up to 1 week.

Use pesto as a dip with some crunchy raw vegies, spread it on crusty bread for a special chicken sandwich, or fold it into scrambled eggs and serve them with bacon for a 'green eggs and ham' breakfast treat!

MIX IT UP
Rocket pesto
Replace the basil and parsley leaves with 100g rocket and use 180ml (¾ cup olive oil) and 60ml (¼ cup) truffle oil.

Pesto dressing
Combine ¼ cup pesto, 2 tbs extra virgin olive oil and 2 tsp lemon juice. Use to drizzle over tomato and ricotta tart (see recipe, page 27) or steamed chat potatoes.

Chilli hummus

MAKES: 2½ CUPS
PREPARATION: 10 MINS

2 x 400g cans chickpeas, rinsed, drained
2 tbs tahini (sesame seed paste, from supermarkets and health food shops)
2 tsp ground cumin
¼ tsp dried chilli flakes
2 cloves garlic, crushed
½ tsp smoked sweet paprika, plus extra, to serve (see Top Tip, page 61)
60ml (¼ cup) lemon juice
60ml (¼ cup) extra virgin olive oil, plus extra, to drizzle

1 Making the hummus
Place chickpeas, tahini, cumin, chilli flakes, garlic, smoked paprika and lemon juice in a food processor and process to a coarse paste. Add oil and 60ml (¼ cup) water, season well with salt and pepper, and process until smooth.

2 Serving the hummus
Transfer hummus to a bowl, sprinkle with extra paprika and drizzle with extra virgin olive oil. Or transfer to an airtight container and refrigerate for up to 1 week. To make a plain hummus, omit the chilli flakes and smoked paprika.

MIX IT UP
Herbed hummus
Place 1 quantity hummus, ⅓ cup finely chopped flat-leaf parsley and 2 tbs chopped mint in a food processor and process until combined. Makes 2¾ cups.

Dukkah

MAKES: 3½ CUPS
PREPARATION: 10 MINS
COOKING: 15 MINS

140g (1 cup) macadamias
140g (1 cup) pistachio kernels
150g (1 cup) sesame seeds
⅓ cup coriander seeds
2 tbs cumin seeds
1 tsp sea salt flakes

1 Roasting the nuts and seeds
Preheat oven to 200C. Place nuts on an oven tray and roast for 8 minutes or until light golden. Set aside to cool. Place sesame seeds in a frying pan over high heat and cook, stirring continuously, for 4 minutes or until light golden. Transfer seeds to a large bowl.

2 Preparing the spices
Place coriander and cumin seeds in a frying pan and stir over medium heat for 2 minutes or until fragrant. Using a mortar and pestle, grind spices to a fine powder. Add spice mixture and salt to the sesame seeds in the bowl. Using a mortar and pestle, coarsely grind the nuts. Add to the bowl and stir to combine. Store dukkah in an airtight container for up to 1 month.

Mezze plate

Serve chilli hummus with a selection of raw and cooked vegetables, sliced crusty bread or toasted flatbread, with dukkah and extra virgin olive oil for dipping.

MY SCORE /10

This chilli jam is delicious served on a steak sandwich or with chargrilled seafood, meat or vegetables.

Chilli jam

MAKES: 1½ CUPS
PREPARATION: 20 MINS
COOKING: 1 HR 5 MINS

1kg (4 small) red capsicums, halved, seeds and membrane removed
1 tbs olive oil
1 small red onion, finely chopped
3 cloves garlic, crushed
6 long red chillies*, seeded, finely chopped
200g (1 cup firmly packed) brown sugar
80ml (⅓ cup) balsamic vinegar
2 tbs fish sauce
1 tbs lime juice

1 Preparing the capsicums

Preheat a grill to high. Line an oven tray with foil and place capsicums, skin-side up, on tray. Transfer to grill and cook for 10 minutes or until skins blister and blacken. Remove tray, fold over foil to enclose capsicums and set aside for 5 minutes to cool slightly. When cool enough to handle, peel skins and discard, then roughly chop capsicums.

2 Cooking the vegetable mixture

Heat oil in a large saucepan over medium–high heat. Cook onion for 2 minutes or until starting to soften. Add garlic and chillies, and cook for 1 minute. Reduce heat to medium. Add capsicums, sugar and vinegar and stir until sugar dissolves. Bring mixture to a simmer and cook, stirring occasionally, for 50 minutes or until thick and sticky. Stir in fish sauce and lime juice. Cool.

3 Finishing the chilli jam

Pulse mixture in a food processor until combined but retaining some texture. Transfer the chilli jam to sterilised jars, then seal (see Chef's Tip). The chilli jam will keep, refrigerated, for up to 1 month.

Chef's Tip

To sterilise jars, preheat oven to 100C. Wash jars and lids in hot, soapy water, then rinse and place in a deep saucepan. Cover with cold water and bring to the boil. Cover, reduce heat and simmer for 10 minutes. Using tongs, place jars and lids upside-down on an oven tray lined with a tea towel. Dry in the oven for 15 minutes. Always place hot mixture in hot jars and cold mixture in cold jars.

TOP TIP

* The recipe produces a mild jam, so if you like it hotter, leave the seeds in when preparing the chillies.

Berry compote

MAKES: 2 CUPS
PREPARATION: 10 MINS
COOKING: 5 MINS

1 lemon
1 vanilla bean
600g frozen mixed
  berries, defrosted
110g (½ cup) caster
  sugar
1 cinnamon quill
2 tsp cornflour

1 Zesting the lemon
Using a vegetable peeler, peel zest from lemon in wide strips. Reserve lemon for another use.

2 Cooking the compote
Place vanilla bean on a chopping board. Using a small, sharp knife, split vanilla bean in half lengthwise. Using the dull side of the knife, scrape along each cut half, collecting the seeds on the knife tip, then place seeds and bean in a saucepan with lemon zest, berries, sugar and cinnamon. Stir over low heat until sugar dissolves, then cook, stirring occasionally, for a further 2 minutes or until berries soften.

3 Finishing the compote
Combine cornflour and 1 tbs water in a small bowl and stir until smooth. Add cornflour mixture to the berry mixture in the pan. Increase heat to medium and cook, stirring occasionally, for 2 minutes or until mixture thickens. Discard lemon zest, cinnamon quill and vanilla bean. Serve berry compote warm, or refrigerate in an airtight container for up to 1 week.

BERRY CRUMBLE

Preheat oven to 180C. Combine 75g (½ cup) plain flour, 75g (⅓ cup firmly packed) brown sugar and 50g chilled chopped unsalted butter in a bowl. Using your fingertips, rub butter into flour mixture until mixture resembles breadcrumbs. Add 70g (½ cup) roughly chopped macadamias and stir to combine. Divide compote among 4 x 180ml (¾-cup) ovenproof dishes. Top with crumble mixture and bake for 20 minutes or until crumble topping is golden.

Berry compote with crêpes

For a yummy breakfast or dessert, make the crêpe recipe on page 39, adding 2 tbs caster sugar to the batter. Serve with berry compote and a dollop of Greek-style yoghurt or double cream.

MY SCORE   /10

Hot chocolate fudge sauce

MAKES: 2 CUPS
PREPARATION: 5 MINS
COOKING: 3 MINS

200g dark chocolate
    (70% cocoa solids
    – see Chef's Tip),
    chopped
250ml (1 cup)
    thickened cream
2 tbs brown sugar
1 tbs golden syrup
30g butter

1 Making the sauce
Place chocolate, cream, sugar, syrup and butter in a small saucepan. Stir over low heat for 3 minutes or until chocolate is melted and combined. Serve hot chocolate fudge sauce immediately, as it will thicken and set as it cools.

Chef's Tip Cocoa solids give chocolate its flavour, so dark chocolate has a much higher percentage than milk chocolate. Choose a product that contains 55%–85% cocoa solids, depending on how bitter you like your chocolate. Avoid chocolate with any added butter or oil, as it's not suitable for use in cooking.

MIX IT UP

Banana split (opposite)
Peel and cut a banana in half lengthwise. Place each half in a small bowl with a scoop of vanilla ice-cream and drizzle with hot chocolate fudge sauce. Top with chopped Toblerone, chopped roasted almonds and half a strawberry. Serves 2.

Chocolate sundae
Layer alternate scoops of vanilla and chocolate ice-cream in a glass, drizzle with hot chocolate fudge sauce and scatter with chopped roasted almonds.

about
LiTTLe
BiTeS
Popcorn

Filo pastry is available, refrigerated or frozen, from supermarkets. We use refrigerated filo, as it doesn't need time to defrost and is easier to work with.

LESSON 1
Working with rice paper wrappers

1 To soak rice paper wrappers, fill a large bowl one-third full with lukewarm water. Working with one rice paper wrapper at a time, place in the water and leave it to soak for 30 seconds or until softened. Transfer wrapper to a clean tea towel spread on a work surface (the tea towel will absorb any excess water). The wrapper is now ready to fill and roll. Repeat with remaining rice paper wrappers.

2 To fill rice paper wrappers, place filling widthwise across the wrapper, 3cm from the edge nearest you. Fold the bottom edge of the wrapper up and over the filling, roll over once, then fold in one side to enclose the filling. Continue rolling to form a tight roll. You can tuck in herbs such as Thai basil or garlic chives into the unrolled flap so that they stick out slightly from the end of the roll. Transfer finished roll to a plate and cover with a slightly damp clean tea towel (see Lesson #2, right), or cover with plastic wrap. Repeat process with remaining rice paper wrappers and filling.

LESSON 2
Working with filo

1 Because filo dries out quickly and becomes brittle, it needs to be kept covered. Using your fingertips, flick a little water onto a clean tea towel, then wring it out so that it is slightly damp all over. Remove the roll of filo sheets from the packet, unroll it and place flat on a clean, dry work surface. Cover filo with the dampened tea towel. Work with one sheet at a time, keeping the rest covered. If the top sheet of filo is a little too moist, use the next sheet down.

2 Grease an oven tray with melted butter or olive oil. Then, working with one sheet at a time, brush filo with melted butter or olive olive and place in tray. Repeat brushing and layering filo sheets until you have the required amount for the recipe. If you are making a covered pie, brush the top layer of filo with melted butter or olive oil before baking in the oven.

Beef quesadillas

SERVES: 4
PREPARATION: 10 MINS
COOKING: 15 MINS

100ml olive oil
1 onion, finely chopped
500g minced beef
35g sachet taco
   seasoning mix
400g can red kidney
   beans, rinsed, drained
2 tbs finely chopped
   coriander leaves
   and stems*
1 tbs sweet chilli sauce
8 x 20cm flour tortillas
120g (1 cup)
   grated cheddar
Rocket, lime wedges,
   sour cream and sweet
   chilli sauce, to serve

1 Cooking the beef mixture

Heat 1 tbs oil in a large frying pan over medium–high heat. Add onion and cook, stirring frequently, for 5 minutes or until soft. Add mince and cook for 4 minutes or until browned, breaking up any lumps with a wooden spoon. Add taco seasoning mix and stir for 30 seconds to combine. Add kidney beans, coriander and sweet chilli sauce and stir to combine. Cool beef mixture slightly.

2 Assembling the quesadillas

Place 4 tortillas on a clean work surface and top each with a heaped ½ cup of beef mixture, leaving a 2cm border. Sprinkle each with 30g (¼ cup) cheddar and cover with the remaining tortillas, pressing down gently with the palm of your hand.

3 Cooking the quesadillas

Preheat oven to 150C. Line an oven tray with baking paper. Heat 1 tbs oil in a frying pan over medium heat and cook a quesadilla for 1 minute or until lightly browned underneath. Using a metal spatula, carefully turn over quesadilla and cook for a further 30 seconds or until lightly browned and cheese has melted. Transfer to the prepared oven tray and keep warm in oven. Repeat with remaining oil and quesadillas.

4 Serving the quesadillas

Cut quesadillas into quarters, then serve with rocket, lime wedges, sour cream and sweet chilli sauce.

TOP TIP

* Coriander is known as cilantro in Mexico, where it features in salads and salsas. Both the leaves and stems are used. In Asian cookery, the roots are also used in curry pastes.

MY SCORE /10

MY SCORE   /10

Ham & gruyère croissants

SERVES: 4
PREPARATION: 5 MINS
COOKING: 10 MINS

4 medium frozen
   croissants, thawed
   (see Chef's Tip)
75g (¼ cup) mayonnaise
   (see Staples, page 6)
2 tsp Dijon mustard
50g shaved ham
60g (½ cup) grated
   gruyère*

1 Preparing the croissants

Preheat oven to 200C. Using a small, serrated knife, cut the croissants in half horizontally. Combine mayonnaise and mustard in a small bowl. Spread mayonnaise mixture over the cut side of the bottom half of each croissant. Divide ham and cheese among croissant bases, then sandwich with the croissant tops.

2 Baking the croissants

Place filled croissants on an oven tray and bake for 8 minutes or until crisp and cheese has melted. Serve immediately.

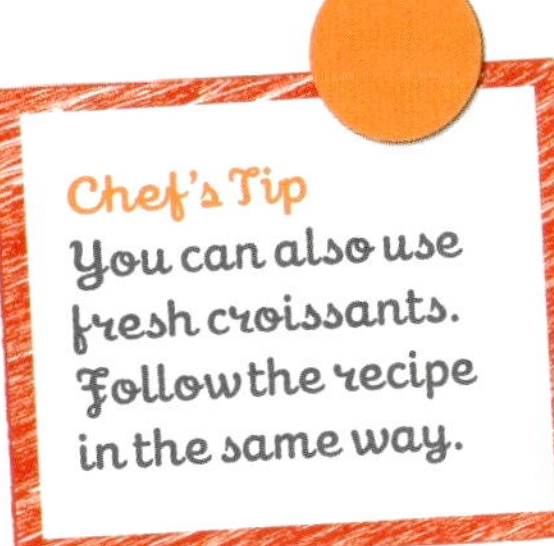

Chef's Tip
You can also use fresh croissants. Follow the recipe in the same way.

For chocolate croissants, preheat oven to 200C. Using a small, serrated knife, cut the croissants in half horizontally, then place 3 squares of milk or plain chocolate on the bottom half, sandwich with the top and bake for 8 minutes until chocolate melts – yum!

TOP TIP
* Gruyère is a firm Swiss cow's milk cheese from a town of the same name – Gruyères – in Switzerland. It has a sweet, nutty taste and melts well. It's available from delis and supermarkets. Substitute cheddar.

Chicken rice paper rolls

SERVES: 4
PREPARATION: 20 MINS

50g rice vermicelli
noodles
1 Lebanese cucumber
160g (1 cup) shredded
barbecue chicken
¼ cup coriander leaves
4 eschalots, thinly sliced
35g (¼ cup) roasted
unsalted peanuts,
roughly chopped
2 tbs hoisin sauce
1 tbs plum sauce
8 x 21cm rice paper
wrappers (see
Chef's Tips)

Dipping sauce
80ml (⅓ cup)
plum sauce
2 tbs hoisin sauce
1 tbs lime juice

1 Making the dipping sauce

To make the dipping sauce, place all ingredients in a small bowl and stir to combine. Set aside.

2 Preparing the noodles

Place noodles in a heatproof bowl and pour over enough boiling water to cover. Stand for 5 minutes, then drain. Meanwhile, cut cucumber in half lengthwise, then cut each half lengthwise into 4 long wedges. Cut wedges in half widthwise. Using scissors, cut noodles into shorter lengths (this will help them to combine with the other ingredients more evenly).

3 Combining the ingredients

Place noodles, cucumber, chicken, coriander, eschalots and peanuts in a bowl. Add hoisin and plum sauces and toss to combine.

4 Assembling the rolls

To soak rice paper wrappers, fill a large bowl one-third full with lukewarm water. Place a rice paper wrapper in the water and leave it to soak for 30 seconds or until softened. Transfer it to a clean tea towel spread on a work surface (the tea towel will absorb any excess water). The wrapper is now ready to fill (see Lesson #1, page 19). Place ⅓ cup of filling mixture 3cm from the edge nearest you. Fold the bottom edge of the wrapper up and over the filling, roll over once, then fold in one side to enclose the filling. Continue rolling to form a tight roll. Transfer finished roll to a plate and cover with a slightly damp clean tea towel (see Lesson #2, page 19). Repeat with remaining rice paper wrappers and filling to make 8 rolls. Serve with dipping sauce.

Chef's Tips

* If you want smaller rolls, use 16 x 16cm rice paper wrappers and fill each with 2 tbs chicken mixture.

* To save time, as you remove one soaked rice paper from water, place another one in the bowl. It will have softened by the time you need it.

MY SCORE /10

MY SCORE   /10

Tomato and ricotta tart

SERVES: 4–6
PREPARATION: 20 MINS
COOKING: 55 MINS

275g small truss
  tomatoes*
2 tbs extra virgin
  olive oil
200g fresh ricotta
120g (½ cup) cream
  cheese, at room
  temperature
80g (⅓ cup) sour cream
1 egg, lightly beaten
1 egg yolk
6 sheets filo pastry
60g butter, melted
200g bocconcini, torn
¼ cup basil leaves, torn
65g (¼ cup) pesto
  dressing (see Staples,
  page 9)

1 Roasting the tomatoes
Preheat oven to 200C. Line an oven tray with baking paper, then place tomatoes on tray and drizzle with oil. Season with salt and pepper. Roast for 15 minutes or until tomatoes are slightly wrinkly. Remove from oven and set aside. Reduce oven to 180C.

2 Making the ricotta mixture
Meanwhile, place ricotta, cream cheese, sour cream, egg and egg yolk in a bowl. Using a wooden spoon, beat mixture until smooth and combined. Season with salt and pepper.

3 Preparing the filo
Lightly grease a 19cm x 27cm non-stick slice pan. Working with one filo sheet at a time, place a sheet of filo on a work surface and lightly brush with melted butter. Cover with another sheet of filo and brush with butter. Repeat stacking and brushing with remaining pastry and butter (see Lesson #2, page 19). Place pastry stack in pan. Fold the pastry sides in to form a neat edge.

4 Layering the filling
Spread ricotta mixture over the tart base. Cut tomatoes from vine and arrange alternately over tart with bocconcini and basil leaves. Season with salt and pepper. Brush pastry edge with remaining melted butter.

5 Baking the tart
Place tart pan on an oven tray and bake for 40 minutes or until pastry is golden and ricotta mixture is set. Serve slices of tart drizzled with pesto dressing.

TOP TIP

* Tomatoes grow on branches known as trusses or vines. If you can't find small truss tomatoes, use large cherry tomatoes instead. Did you know that a tomato is really a fruit, and that it wasn't until the 18th century that the British started to eat them, initially believing them to be poisonous?

about
Eggs

LESSON 3
Blowtorch method

This method creates a crisp, caramelised sugar crust for a crème brûlée. Always have an adult to help you, as a blowtorch can be dangerous to use. Place the chilled brûlées on an oven tray, preferably on a stove top or non-flammable benchtop. Light the blowtorch, hold it approximately 5cm from the brûlée and move it backwards and forwards over the top, until the sugar has melted and caramelised. It's important to keep the flame moving or the sugar will burn. It's also important to work quite quickly so you don't heat up the custard underneath too much. If this happens, the custard may split, becoming grainy and watery. If you want a really crunchy layer of caramel, repeat with a second layer of sugar and caramelise again. Experiment with different sugars to find the one you prefer: try caster, brown or raw sugar. Pastry blowtorches are available from kitchenware stores.

To make a round meringue, use a pencil to trace around a plate or bowl the size you require on a sheet of baking paper, then turn over the paper. Dollop the egg-white mixture in the middle, then spread it out with a palette knife or the back of a spoon to fill inside the pencilled line.

LESSON 4
Making meringue

Separate egg whites from yolks, then add to a clean mixing bowl. Start by whisking with an electric mixer on low–medium until frothy, then on high speed until soft peaks form (when the beaters are lifted, the egg white rises, but the peaks collapse). Whisk until glossy and stiff peaks form (when the beaters are lifted, the peaks stay pointing straight up and don't collapse). 'Weeping' meringues (when clear drops of liquid sugar appear) are caused by under- or over-beating the whites. You can avoid this by beating in some cornflour after adding the sugar.

Twice-baked cheese soufflés

SERVES: 6
PREPARATION: 15 MINS
COOKING: 30 MINS

430ml (1¾ cups) milk
¼ small onion,
   roughly chopped
2 bay leaves
60g butter, chopped,
   plus extra soft butter,
   to grease
50g (⅓ cup) plain flour
40g (½ cup) finely
   grated parmesan
60g (½ cup) finely
   grated gruyère
   (see Top Tip, page 23)
3 egg yolks, at
   room temperature
4 egg whites, at
   room temperature
1 tbs chopped chives,
   to serve

Cheese sauce
250ml (1 cup)
   pouring cream
40g (⅓ cup) finely
   grated gruyère
   (see Top Tip, page 23)

1 Infusing the milk
Preheat oven to 170C. Grease 6 x 180ml (¾-cup) ovenproof ramekins. Place milk, onion and bay leaves in a small saucepan and bring to a simmer over medium heat. Remove from heat and set aside for 10 minutes for flavours to infuse, then strain over a jug. Discard onion and bay leaves.

2 Making the cheese sauce
Meanwhile, melt butter in a saucepan over medium heat. Add flour and cook for 1 minute or until grainy. Remove from heat and gradually stir in milk until smooth. Return to heat and stir continuously for 1 minute or until mixture boils and thickens. Stir in cheeses until melted. Transfer cheese sauce to a bowl, then add egg yolks and stir until combined.

3 Folding egg whites into cheese mixture
Using an electric mixer, whisk egg whites until soft peaks form (see Lesson #4, page 29). Using a large metal spoon, add half the egg whites to the cheese mixture and fold in until mixture is loosened, then fold in the remaining egg whites until just combined (don't over-mix, as you want to preserve as much air as possible in the egg whites).

4 Baking the soufflés
Divide cheese mixture among ramekins and place ramekins in a roasting pan. Carefully pour in enough boiling water to come halfway up the side of the dishes (get an adult to help you do this as well as place them in and take them out of the oven). Bake for 20 minutes or until puffed and golden. Wearing oven gloves, remove ramekins from water bath and cool for 10 minutes. Taking care, as the ramekins will still be hot, run a knife around the inner edge of each soufflé to loosen, then invert into shallow ovenproof dishes.

5 Making the sauce
Increase oven to 190C. To make sauce, combine cream and cheese in a small bowl. Pour over each soufflé. Bake for 10 minutes or until golden. Sprinkle with chopped chives and serve immediately.

Chef's Tip You can make the soufflés to the end of step 4 and refrigerate for up to 1 day.

Grease your ramekins by brushing them with soft butter in an upwards motion – from the base to the rim. This helps the soufflé mixture to rise even better!

MY SCORE /10

MY SCORE   /10

Chorizo tortilla

SERVES: 6
PREPARATION: 15 MINS
COOKING: 25 MINS

500g desiree potatoes
(or other waxy
potatoes, such
as nicola), peeled,
thinly sliced
1 tbs olive oil
2 dried chorizo
sausages,* thinly sliced
1 onion, thinly sliced
½ tsp smoked paprika
(see Top Tip, page 61)
8 eggs

1 Cooking the potatoes
Bring a saucepan of
salted water to the boil
and par-cook potatoes
for 5 minutes or until just
tender. Drain and pat dry
with paper towel.

2 Frying the chorizo
Heat oil in a 23cm
(base measurement)
frying pan. Add chorizo
and cook, stirring, for
2 minutes or until lightly
browned. Using a slotted
spoon, transfer to a
plate. Add onion to the
pan and cook, stirring
frequently, for 5 minutes
or until soft. Add paprika
and cook for 30 seconds.
Transfer onion mixture
to a bowl. Reserve pan.

3 Assembling the tortilla
Preheat a grill to
medium–high. Layer
onion mixture, potatoes,
and chorizo alternately
in the frying pan,
seasoning with salt
and pepper as you layer.
Crack eggs into a bowl,
then whisk until smooth.
Pour eggs into the frying
pan and cook tortilla
over low heat for
5 minutes or until base
and side of tortilla are
just set. Remove from
heat, place under the
grill and cook for
a further 7 minutes
or until the top is set.

4 Serving the tortilla
Using a small spatula,
loosen the edge and
base of the tortilla, then
slide onto a plate (get
an adult to help you).
Alternatively, serve
tortilla straight from
the pan. Cut tortilla
into wedges to serve.

Waxy potatoes are the best ones to use for this dish, as they hold their shape and don't go 'mushy' if slightly overcooked. You can also add herbs such as basil and oregano for some extra flavour.

TOP TIP

* Chorizo is a spicy pork sausage originating from Spain, flavoured with paprika and garlic. In its fresh form, it's sold with other sausages, but when it's aged (and is drier and harder), it is sold in the deli section of supermarkets.

Crème brûlée

SERVES: 4
PREPARATION: 10 MINS
COOKING: 50 MINS
Allow 4 hours to chill the custards.

500ml (2 cups) pouring cream
1 vanilla bean
6 egg yolks
55g (¼ cup) caster sugar, plus 2 tbs extra, to sprinkle

1 Infusing the cream
Preheat oven to 150C. Place cream in a saucepan. Place vanilla bean on a chopping board. Using a small, sharp knife, split vanilla bean in half lengthwise. Using the dull side of the knife, scrape along each cut half, collecting the seeds on the knife tip, then add seeds and bean to the cream. Bring cream mixture almost to the boil over high heat, then reduce heat to low-medium and simmer for 2 minutes. Discard vanilla bean and pour cream into a jug.

2 Making the custard
Place egg yolks and 55g (¼ cup) sugar in a heatproof bowl and whisk until combined. Whisking continuously, gradually pour in the hot cream until combined.

3 Cooking the custard
Divide egg yolk mixture among 4 x 160ml (⅔-cup) ramekins. Place ramekins in a roasting pan and carefully pour in enough boiling water to come halfway up the side of the dishes (get an adult to help you do this, as well as place them in and take them out of the oven). Bake, uncovered, for 40 minutes or until set. Set aside to cool.

Remove custards from the water bath, cover with plastic wrap and refrigerate for at least 4 hours or overnight until chilled.

4 Caramelising the custards
Preheat grill to high. Place ramekins in a roasting pan and surround with ice cubes. Sprinkle the top of each custard with 2 tsp extra caster sugar. Place pan under the grill and cook for 4 minutes or until sugar caramelises. Refrigerate for up to 1 hour or until ready to serve.

> Placing the ramekins in a roasting pan with ice cubes prevents the custard from heating up too much under the grill, which might cause it to 'split' or separate.

TOP TIP
* Crème brûlée means 'burnt cream' in French and refers to the caramelised top on this custard dessert. There are two ways you can do this: under the grill, or with a pastry blowtorch (see Lesson #3, page 29).

MY SCORE   /10

MY SCORE   /10

Chocolate hazelnut layered pavlova

SERVES: 8
PREPARATION: 20 MINS
COOKING: 50 MINS
Allow an extra 3 hours for pavlovas to cool.

6 egg whites, at
    room temperature
330g (1½ cups)
    caster sugar
20g (¼ cup) Dutch
    cocoa (see Chef's
    Tip) sifted
125g ground hazelnuts
600ml thickened cream
150g dark chocolate
    (70% cocoa solids),
    melted (see Lesson
    #15, page 103), plus
    10g dark chocolate,
    extra, grated
300g raspberries
50g roasted hazelnuts,
    chopped

1 Preparing the oven trays
Preheat oven to 140C. Line 2 oven trays with baking paper. Place a 22cm plate or bowl in the centre of the paper, then, using a pencil, trace around the plate to mark a 22cm round. Repeat on second tray. Turn baking paper over so pencil side is underneath.

2 Making the meringue
Using an electric mixer, whisk egg whites to soft peaks (see Lesson #4, page 29). With the motor running, gradually add sugar, 1 tbs at a time. Once you've added 6 tbs sugar, add remainder in a steady stream and whisk until thick and glossy. Be careful not to over-beat or the meringue will become grainy. Combine cocoa and ground hazelnuts in a small bowl, then, using a metal spoon, gently fold into meringue.

3 Baking the meringue
Spoon meringue mixture inside marked rounds on trays and spread to fill rounds, smoothing the top. Bake for 50 minutes or until crisp and hollow-sounding when they're tapped. Turn off oven. Using a wooden spoon, prop oven door ajar and leave pavlovas in the oven to cool for 3 hours.

4 Assembling the pavlova
Using an electric mixer, whisk cream to soft peaks (see Lesson #4, page 29). Place one meringue on a platter and spread with half the cream, then drizzle with half the melted chocolate. Scatter half the raspberries over the chocolate, then top with the second meringue. Spread with remaining cream and drizzle with remaining melted chocolate. Scatter over remaining raspberries and hazelnuts, and sprinkle with extra grated chocolate to serve.

Chef's Tip
Dutch cocoa, from selected supermarkets and delis, has a more concentrated flavour and deeper colour than regular cocoa.

Eggs need to be at room temperature when making meringue so they incorporate plenty of air. If you need to bring them up to room temperature quickly, place eggs in a bowl of warm water for 5 minutes.

I'm so impressed overall.
These smoked salmon
crêpes are perfect.
GARY MEHIGAN
MY SCORE   /10

Gracie
Smoked salmon crêpe cakes

SERVES: 6
PREPARATION: 20 MINS
COOKING: 20 MINS
You will need 6 x 125ml
(½-cup) ramekins or
dariole moulds. Allow
3 hours for setting.

Olive oil spray, to grease
400g sliced smoked
   salmon
500g cream cheese,
   at room temperature
2 tbs milk
2 tsp capers, drained,
   finely chopped
1 lemon, zested, juiced
¼ cup finely chopped
   chives
2 tbs olive oil

Crêpe batter
3 eggs
250ml (1 cup) milk
105g (¾ cup) plain flour
80g butter, melted

1 To make crêpe batter, process all ingredients and a pinch of salt in a food processor until smooth. Transfer to a bowl, cover with plastic wrap and set aside for 30 minutes.

2 Spray a 22cm crêpe pan or non-stick frying pan with oil, then heat over low–medium heat. Add 60ml (¼ cup) batter to pan and swirl to thinly coat base (get an adult to help you). Cook for 1½ minutes or until edge of crêpe is light brown. Using a spatula, loosen crêpe, then carefully turn over. Cook for a further 30 seconds or until the underside starts to brown, then transfer to a plate. Repeat with remaining batter to make 6 crêpes.

3 To make filling, roughly chop 100g smaller smoked salmon slices and place in the bowl of an electric mixer. Add cream cheese, milk, capers and lemon zest and 2 tsp juice, and 2 tbs chives. Season with salt and pepper, then beat until well combined.

4 To assemble, line 6 ramekins with plastic wrap so that it overhangs the edge enough to cover the top when folded in. Line each ramekin with a crêpe so that edge overhangs. Line each crêpe shell with slices of smoked salmon, then place filling in the centre. Fold in edge of crêpes to enclose filling, then fold in plastic wrap to cover. Refrigerate for 3 hours or until set.

5 Stir olive oil and remaining 1 tbs chives together in a small bowl. Peel back plastic wrap from the top of ramekins, then turn out crêpe cakes onto plates. Peel away plastic wrap and discard. Serve smoked salmon crêpe cakes drizzled with chive oil.

ABOUT GRACIE
Gracie, aged 12, is from Tasmania and, as well as being a passionate cook, she's a keen hockey player and a dab hand at the flute. She's gluten intolerant, and her ambition is to open a restaurant where everything on the menu is gluten-free. In the egg challenge, she put up two dishes, but it was this one that landed her in the top three.

ABOUT KIEREN

Eleven-year-old Kieren lives in Victoria and comes from a family of cooks – his grandfather was a chef – and his mum started teaching him when he was very young. He comes from a Greek background and loves George Calombaris – of course! This dish wowed the judges in the breakfast in bed challenge.

Kieren
Goat's cheese & honey doughnuts

SERVES: 4
PREPARATION: 15 MINS
COOKING: 5 MINS

55g (¼ cup) caster sugar
½ tsp ground cinnamon
Vegetable oil, to
    shallow-fry
½ (900g) rockmelon,
    flesh cut into 5mm
    pieces
60g soft goat's cheese
    (see Chef's Tip),
    crumbled
50g (½ cup) walnuts,
    finely chopped
2 tbs honey, warmed

Doughnuts
255g (1¾ cups)
    self-raising flour
1 egg
250ml (1 cup) milk

1 To make doughnuts, sift flour and a pinch of salt into a large bowl. Make a well in the centre. Whisk egg and milk together in a jug, then pour into the well. Using a wooden spoon, stir to form a smooth batter.

2 Combine sugar and cinnamon on a large plate. Heat 1cm oil in a large frying pan over medium heat. Working in 2 batches, gently drop 6 heaped tablespoons of batter into the pan (get an adult to help you). Cook doughnuts for 2 minutes each side or until light golden. Using a slotted spoon, remove from the pan, drain on paper towel, then toss in the cinnamon mixture to coat. Repeat with remaining batter to make 12 doughnuts.

3 Divide doughnuts among plates, scatter with rockmelon, goat's cheese and walnuts, and drizzle with warmed honey to serve.

Chef's Tip
If you find the taste of goat's cheese too strong, subsitute ricotta.

The only reason I'm not finishing this is because I want to tell you how delicious it is!
ANNA GARE
MY SCORE   /10

about
PaSta
& RiCe

While arborio rice is the most widely available risotto rice (from supermarkets), carnaroli or vialone nano rice have a higher starch content, which gives the finished risotto an even creamier texture. They're available from delis.

LESSON 5
Making fresh pasta

1 Place 300g (2 cups) '00' flour (from supermarkets), 3 eggs, 1 tbs olive oil and a pinch of salt in a food processor. Process until mixture forms a ball. Briefly knead dough on a lightly floured surface until smooth. Shape into a disc, wrap in plastic wrap and rest at room temperature for 30 minutes.

2 Divide dough into 4 discs. Keeping remainder covered, pass 1 disc through a pasta machine on widest setting (6). Fold in half lengthwise and repeat process, without changing settings. Cut pasta if too long. Repeat process, narrowing settings one notch at a time, until you reach the finest setting (1).

LESSON 6
Making risotto

Risotto should be stirred continuously, and the stock added a ladleful at a time. Allow the stock to be absorbed by the rice before adding another ladleful; the whole process will take about 20 minutes, and the rice should still be slightly al dente (see Chef's Tip, page 44). Add a generous amount of chopped butter and grated parmesan, cover pan with a lid and leave for 2 minutes, then stir to combine. When you serve the risotto, it should flow like molten lava. If it is too firm, add some more stock. As risotto cools quickly, it's best to serve it on warmed plates.

Spaghetti with garlic, lemon & chilli

SERVES: 4
PREPARATION: 10 MINS
COOKING: 10 MINS

125ml (½ cup) extra
   virgin olive oil
2 onions, finely chopped
4 cloves garlic, very
   thinly sliced
1 long red chilli, seeded,
   finely chopped
250g spaghetti
2 tomatoes, seeded,
   finely chopped
¼ cup finely chopped
   flat-leaf parsley
1 lemon, zested
Crisp capers (see recipe
   below) and lemon
   wedges, to serve

1 Cooking the onions, garlic and chilli
Heat oil in a large, deep frying pan over low heat. Add onions, garlic and chilli, and cook, stirring occasionally, for 10 minutes or until onions are soft.

2 Cooking the pasta
Meanwhile, cook pasta in a saucepan of boiling salted water for 10 minutes or until al dente (see Chef's Tip). Drain over a bowl and reserve 60ml (¼ cup) of the pasta cooking water.

3 Tossing the pasta
Add pasta to the onion mixture with reserved pasta cooking water, tomatoes, parsley and lemon zest. Using tongs, toss until well combined. Season with salt and pepper.

4 Serving the pasta
Divide pasta among bowls, scatter with crisp capers and serve with lemon wedges to squeeze over pasta.

Chef's Tip Al dente means 'to the bite' in Italian. Perfectly cooked pasta should still have a little resistance when you bite into it.

There's no need to add oil to the saucepan when cooking pasta, as it will just get washed down the sink when it's drained. Instead, give the pasta a quick stir in the pan with long tongs or a slotted spoon when you first place it in the boiling salted water.

CRISP CAPERS

Heat 2 tbs olive oil in a frying pan over medium heat and cook 65g (⅓ cup) drained capers, stirring, for 5 minutes or until crisp. Drain on paper towel.

MY SCORE   /10

MY SCORE   /10

Pumpkin pilaf

SERVES: 6–8
PREPARATION: 20 MINS
COOKING: 25 MINS

80ml (⅓ cup) olive oil
1 (500g) large eggplant, cut into 2cm cubes
20g butter
1 red onion, finely chopped
2 cloves garlic, crushed
1 tsp ground cumin*
2 tsp ground coriander*
1 cinnamon quill*
400g (2 cups) basmati rice, rinsed well
1L (4 cups) chicken stock
450g peeled, seeded, butternut pumpkin, cut into 1.5cm cubes (see Lesson #8, page 57)
50g (¼ cup) currants
80g unsalted pistachio kernels, roasted, chopped
¾ cup chopped coriander leaves

1 Frying the eggplant
Heat 60ml (¼ cup) olive oil in a large, deep frying pan with a lid. Add eggplant and cook, stirring frequently, for 7 minutes or until golden and softened. Transfer to a bowl and set aside.

2 Cooking the pumpkin mixture
Heat butter and remaining 1 tbs oil in the same pan over medium heat. Add onion and cook for 2 minutes or until slightly softened. Add garlic and spices, and cook, stirring, for 1 minute or until fragrant. Add rice, stock and pumpkin, and stir to combine. Season with salt and pepper.

3 Cooking the pilaf
Bring the pumpkin mixture to the boil. Add currants and eggplant, and stir to combine. Reduce heat to low, cover with a lid and cook for 15 minutes or until liquid is absorbed. Stand, covered, for a further 5 minutes. Scatter pistachios and coriander over pilaf and serve immediately.

Basmati is a delicately fragrant long-grain rice, chiefly grown in India, Pakistan and Bangladesh (as well as Australia!). It can be fluffed and separated easily, and is the traditional variety used for dishes such as pilaf.

TOP TIPS
* Cumin and coriander seeds are staples in Indian cooking and are usually toasted, then ground together as part of a spice mixture. Cumin has an earthy, warm scent and flavour, while coriander has a more floral, citrus tang.
* Cinnamon is made from the inner bark of the cinnamomum tree. It has a warm, spicy fragrance and flavour, and is used in both savoury and sweet dishes.

Four-cheese gnocchi bake

SERVES: 4
PREPARATION: 10 MINS
COOKING: 30 MINS

500g store-bought
  potato gnocchi
30g butter, plus 10g
  extra, finely chopped
3 tsp plain flour
300ml thickened cream
100g gorgonzola,*
  crumbled
160g provolone,* grated
150g gruyère,* grated
30g (½ cup) fresh
  breadcrumbs
2 tbs finely grated
  parmesan
1 tbs finely chopped
  flat-leaf parsley
Pear and rocket
  salad, to serve
  (see Chef's Tip)

1 Cooking the gnocchi
Bring a large saucepan of water to the boil. Add gnocchi and cook for 5 minutes or until they float to the surface. Drain. Set aside.

2 Making the sauce
Preheat oven to 190C. Melt butter in a large saucepan over medium–high heat. Add flour and cook, stirring, for 30 seconds or until grainy. Gradually stir in cream and bring almost to the boil. Remove from heat and stir in gorgonzola, provolone and gruyère. Return to a low heat and stir for 1 minute or until combined. Season with salt and pepper.

3 Baking the gnocchi
Divide gnocchi among 4 x 375ml (1½-cup) ovenproof dishes, then spoon over the sauce. Combine breadcrumbs, parmesan and parsley in a small bowl. Sprinkle crumb mixture over gnocchi and dot with extra chopped butter. Bake for 20 minutes or until golden. Serve immediately with pear and rocket salad.

Chef's Tip This is a rich bake, so serve it with a light, refreshing salad. Sweet pear and peppery rocket are a perfect match.

TOP TIPS

* Gorgonzola is an Italian blue-vein cow's milk cheese sold at different stages of maturity. The young, sweet version is labelled *dolce* and, as it becomes more pungent, is sold as *piccante*.
* Provolone is also an Italian cow's milk cheese, made similarly to mozzarella, except the exterior is hand-rubbed with brine before the cheese is hung to age and dry. For more details on gruyère, see Top Tip, page 23. These cheeses are available from selected supermarkets and delis.

MY SCORE /10

This dish is packed with flavour and the presentation is just amazing.
ALESSANDRO PAVONI
MY SCORE   /10

Hannah
Chicken & leek ravioli with brown butter

SERVES: 4 (MAKES 20)
PREPARATION: 45 MINS
COOKING: 30 MINS

500g rock salt
500g baby roma
   tomatoes, halved
60ml (¼ cup) olive oil
1 leek, thinly sliced
1 clove garlic, crushed
½ zucchini, grated
30g baby spinach,
   finely chopped
2 tbs finely chopped
   flat-leaf parsley
1 tbs chicken stock
125g light cream
   cheese, softened
1 egg
40g (¼ cup) grated
   Four Cheese Blend
250g minced chicken
4 slices pancetta
100g butter, chopped
10 basil leaves
½ lemon, juiced
Grated parmesan,
   to serve

Pasta dough
375g (2½ cups) '00'
   flour, plus extra,
   to dust
½ tsp salt
4 eggs, lightly beaten
1 tbs olive oil

1 To make pasta dough, follow the method in Step 1, Lesson #5, page 43. After kneading, divide dough into 4 pieces, wrap in plastic wrap and set aside for 30 minutes.

2 Preheat oven to 180C and line an oven tray with rock salt. Place tomatoes, cut-side up, on salt. Roast for 20 minutes or until soft. Set tomatoes aside.

3 Meanwhile, heat 2 tbs oil in a large frying pan over medium heat. Add leek and garlic, and stir for 5 minutes or until leek is soft. Add zucchini, spinach, parsley and stock. Cook, stirring occasionally, for a further 3 minutes or until tender. Transfer to a large bowl and refrigerate for 15 minutes. Add cream cheese, egg, cheese blend and chicken. Season and stir to combine.

4 To roll pasta into 4 sheets, see Step 2, Lesson #5, page 43. To make ravioli, place pasta sheets on a lightly floured work surface. Place 5 heaped tablespoonfuls of filling, 6cm apart, 3cm up from bottom of each sheet. Brush around filling with water, then fold sheet in half lengthwise to enclose. Press gently between filling to remove air pockets. Using a 7cm round cutter, cut out rounds and place on a clean tea towel. Seal edges with a fork.

ABOUT HANNAH

At 10 years of age, Hannah, from Victoria, is the second youngest contestant in the top 20. Her favourite chef is Gary Mehigan, and her dream is to one day open a restaurant on the Mornington Peninsula. This ravioli dish won her a *MasterChef* apron in the Italian challenge – and praise from guest judge Alessandro Pavoni.

5 Cook ravioli in a large saucepan of boiling salted water for 6 minutes or until cooked through. Drain.

6 Meanwhile, heat remaining 1 tbs oil in a small, heavy-based frying pan over medium–high heat. Add pancetta and cook, turning frequently, for 2 minutes or until crisp. Drain on paper towel. Return pan to high heat. Add butter and basil leaves, and cook for 1 minute or until butter turns dark golden. Remove from heat and stir in lemon juice. Divide ravioli among bowls and top with roasted tomatoes, pancetta and basil. Drizzle with brown butter and serve with grated parmesan.

Aya
Black sesame tagliatelle with puttanesca sauce

SERVES: 4
PREPARATION: 40 MINS
COOKING: 15 MINS

60ml (¼ cup) extra
 virgin olive oil
1 onion, finely chopped
2 cloves garlic, crushed
5 anchovy fillets,
 finely chopped
2 tbs tomato paste
400g can Italian
 diced tomatoes
½ cup flat-leaf parsley,
 roughly chopped
12 pitted kalamata
 olives, thinly sliced
45g (¼ cup) baby
 capers, finely chopped
¼ cup basil, roughly
 chopped, plus extra
 leaves, to serve
¼ tsp chilli powder
 (optional)

Pasta dough
2 tbs black sesame
 seeds,* roasted
200g (1⅓ cups)
 '00' flour*
2 eggs
1 egg yolk

1 To make pasta dough, using a mortar and pestle, grind half the sesame seeds to a fine powder. Place in a large bowl with flour. Season with a pinch of salt and stir to combine. Whisk eggs and yolk together in a bowl. Mound flour mixture on a work surface, make a well in centre and add egg mixture. Using a fork, draw in flour until mixture is thick, then, using your hands, work in remaining flour. Knead dough for 6 minutes or until firm; add extra flour if sticky. Wrap dough in plastic wrap and set aside for 30 minutes.

2 To roll pasta into sheets, see Step 2, Lesson #5, page 43. To make tagliatelle, feed each sheet through the tagliatelle cutter. Dust with flour.

3 Heat oil in a large, heavy-based saucepan over high heat. Add onion, garlic and anchovies. Cook, stirring, for 5 minutes or until onion is soft. Stir in remaining ingredients and chilli, if using. Bring to a simmer, then reduce heat to medium and cook, stirring occasionally, for 10 minutes or until thickened. Season with salt and pepper.

4 Cook pasta in a large pan of boiling salted water for 2 minutes or until al dente. Drain. Add to sauce and, using tongs, toss well. Divide pasta among bowls, then scatter with remaining sesame seeds and extra basil to serve.

ABOUT AYA

Aya is 11 years old and comes from New South Wales. She cooks at home most nights of the week. One of her heroes is Sydney chef, Tetsuya Wakuda. Aya would like to be a professional footballer, and this dish certainly scored well – winning her a spot in the top 20!

TOP TIPS

* Black sesame seeds are available from Asian food stores.
* '00' flour is available from supermarkets. It is extra-refined flour used to make pasta.

All of these flavours are in perfect
balance. I don't think I could
improve on that.
GARY MEHIGAN
MY SCORE   /10

You think outside the box – this
would be an amazing vegetable
risotto even without the salmon.
NEIL PERRY
MY SCORE   /10

Jack
Green curry risotto with salmon

SERVES: 4
PREPARATION: 35 MINS
COOKING: 25 MINS

2 long green chillies, seeded, finely chopped
80ml (⅓ cup) light soy sauce
1 tbs brown sugar
1 tbs fish sauce (see Top Tips, page 89)
2 tbs lime juice
4 x 150g skinless pieces salmon fillet
1 tbs vegetable oil
½ cup mixed herbs (Thai basil, mint, coriander)
1 lime, zested, juiced

Curry paste
¼ tsp each ground coriander, cumin and turmeric
5 white peppercorns
1 tsp brown sugar
1 stalk lemongrass (white part only, see Top Tips, page 89), thinly sliced
2 coriander roots
2 tsp grated ginger
2 cloves garlic
1 red eschalot, chopped
2 long green chillies, seeded, chopped
2 kaffir lime leaves (see Top Tips, page 89), finely chopped
1 tsp fish sauce

Risotto
375ml (1½ cups) chicken stock
1 tbs vegetable oil
1 onion, finely chopped
4 kaffir lime leaves, finely shredded
1 tsp grated ginger
1 clove garlic, crushed
200g (1 cup) arborio rice
160ml (⅔ cup) coconut cream

1 Combine chillies, soy, sugar, fish sauce and lime juice in a bowl. Add salmon, toss gently to coat, then cover and set aside at room temperature.

2 To make curry paste, using a mortar and pestle, grind ground spices and peppercorns. Add remaining ingredients and pound to a paste. Makes ⅓ cup.

3 To make risotto, place stock and 310ml (1¼ cups) water in a small saucepan. Bring to the boil, reduce heat to low and keep at a gentle simmer. Heat oil in a saucepan over medium heat. Add onion and stir for 5 minutes or until soft. Stir in 2 tbs curry paste, cook for 30 seconds, then add half the lime leaves, the ginger, garlic and rice, and stir to combine. Add stock 1 cup at a time, stirring until stock is absorbed before adding more (see Lesson #6, page 43). Continue adding stock until rice is cooked but still al dente. Stir in 80ml (⅓ cup) coconut cream. Remove from heat and cover with a lid.

4 Heat 1 tbs oil in a large, non-stick frying pan over medium heat. Drain salmon and cook for 3 minutes each side or until just cooked. Chop half the herbs and stir into risotto with lime zest and 1 tbs juice. Divide risotto among plates and top with salmon. Drizzle with remaining 80ml (⅓ cup) coconut cream and scatter with remaining herbs and lime leaves to serve.

ABOUT JACK
Twelve-year-old Jack is from Queensland. Among his many interests, cooking is his passion. He admits to having a real sweet tooth, and would like to be a successful pastry chef like his hero, Adriano Zumbo. This dish impressed guest judge Neil Perry in the Beverly Hills Mansion challenge in Los Angeles.

about VeGETaBLeS

LESSON 7
Corn & spinach

REMOVING CORN KERNELS First, strip away the husk (green outer casing) and silks (the thin, pale strands) from the corn. Hold the corn cob upright on a board with one hand and, using a sharp knife, cut down the cob between the inner core and kernels, rotating the cob as you go. Try not to cut off any of the core with the kernels as it is very tough.

BLANCHING SPINACH Bring a large saucepan of salted water to the boil. Add spinach and cook for 30 seconds or until just wilted. Drain spinach in a colander, then refresh in iced water and drain again. If you need the spinach to be quite dry, wrap it in a clean tea towel or a couple of layers of paper towel, then gently wring it out.

Pumpkin is very hard to cut, so make sure you get an adult to help you cut it into smaller, more manageable pieces before you peel them and remove the seeds.

LESSON 8
Asparagus & pumpkin

TRIMMING ASPARAGUS To snap off the tough part of asparagus spears, hold the thick end in one hand and the middle of the asparagus in the other. Bend the asparagus towards the thicker end until it snaps (in order to break it as close to the end as possible). Alternatively, trim with a knife.

PEELING AND SEEDING A PUMPKIN Using a sharp knife, place pumpkin on a chopping board and cut into wedges (get an adult to help you). Place a wedge on a chopping board and cut off skin in a downward motion, following the curve of the pumpkin. Alternatively, use a potato peeler. Using a metal spoon, scrape away seeds and the softer, darker strands surrounding them.

Roast pumpkin salad

SERVES: 4
PREPARATION: 10 MINS
COOKING: 30 MINS

1kg jap pumpkin, peeled, seeded, cut into 1.5cm pieces (see Lesson #8, page 57)
12 cloves garlic, unpeeled
2 tbs extra virgin olive oil
1 bunch asparagus, trimmed, halved (see Lesson #8, page 57)
100g baby spinach
1 avocado, halved, stone removed, thinly sliced
50g (⅓ cup) pine nuts, roasted (see Chef's Tip)

Dressing
60ml (¼ cup) extra virgin olive oil
2 tsp sumac*
1 tbs lemon juice
2 tsp honey

1 Roasting the pumpkin and garlic
Preheat oven to 180C. Place pumpkin, garlic and oil in a bowl. Season with salt and pepper, and toss to combine. Transfer to an ovenproof dish and roast for 30 minutes, turning after 20 minutes, or until tender and golden. Cool garlic, then remove skins.

2 Cooking the asparagus
Meanwhile, place asparagus in a bowl and cover with boiling water. Stand for 5 minutes or until asparagus is tender. Drain in a colander, then rinse under cold running water and drain again.

3 Combining the salad ingredients
Place asparagus in a large bowl with pumpkin, garlic, spinach, avocado and pine nuts.

4 Making the dressing
Place all ingredients in a bowl and whisk to combine. Pour dressing over salad, season with salt and pepper, and toss to combine. Divide salad among bowls to serve.

Chef's Tip To roast pine nuts, place in a small frying pan over low-medium heat and stir continuously for 4 minutes or until golden.

TOP TIP
* Sumac is a reddish-brown, sour ground Middle Eastern berry from supermarkets.

MY SCORE   /10

MY SCORE   /10

Mexican corn cobs with smoky mayonnaise

SERVES: 4
PREPARATION: 10 MINS
COOKING: 15 MINS

4 cobs corn, husks
    and silks removed
    (see Chef's Tip)
Olive oil, to brush
75g (⅓ cup) mayonnaise
    (see Staples, page 6)
1 lime, zested
1 small clove garlic,
    crushed
¼ tsp smoked paprika*
80g (⅔ cup) grated
    cheddar
Lime wedges, to serve

1 Chargrilling the corn
Heat a chargrill pan or barbecue over high heat. Brush corn with a little oil and chargrill, turning frequently, for 15 minutes or until lightly charred and tender.

2 Making the smoky mayonnaise
Meanwhile, place mayonnaise, lime zest, garlic and paprika in a small bowl and stir to combine. Season with salt and pepper.

3 Serving the corn
Brush mayonnaise mixture liberally over each corn cob and sprinkle with grated cheese (this will start to melt from the heat of the corn). Season with salt and pepper and serve immediately with lime wedges and remaining smoky mayonnaise.

Chef's Tip To make these look special as we've done for our picture, peel back the husks and tie with kitchen string, then remove the silks.

These corn cobs are delicious on their own, or you could serve them as an accompaniment to barbecued meats or fish.

TOP TIP
* Smoked Spanish paprika (*pimentón*) is made from ground dried red peppers. It comes in several varieties, including sweet (*dulce*), bittersweet (*agridulce*) and hot (*picante*). We've used the sweet variety in our recipes, which is available from supermarkets and specialist food shops.

Trio of fritters

SERVES: 6
PREPARATION: 25 MINS
COOKING: 15 MINS

Vegetable oil,
    to shallow-fry
Mixed-leaf salad, aïoli
    (see Staples, page 6)
    and cucumber
    raita (see Chef's Tip),
    to serve

Potato fritters

400g unpeeled desiree
    potatoes, scrubbed
2 spring onions,
    thinly sliced
1 egg, lightly beaten

Carrot fritters

400g carrots
35g (¼ cup) plain flour
1 tsp ground cumin
2 eggs, lightly beaten

Zucchini fritters

400g zucchinis
60g (¼ cup) firm
    fresh ricotta
35g (¼) cup plain flour
2 eggs, lightly beaten

1 Making the potato fritters

Place potatoes in a saucepan of cold water and bring to the boil. Par-cook for 5 minutes, then drain. Cool. Peel, then coarsely grate potatoes. Combine grated potato, spring onions and egg in a bowl. Season with salt and pepper. Shape into 6 x 10cm rounds, then set aside.

2 Making the carrot fritters

Peel and grate carrots, squeeze out excess liquid and place carrots in a bowl. Add flour and cumin, and stir to combine. Add eggs and stir well to combine. Season with salt and pepper. Shape into 6 x 10cm rounds, then set aside.

3 Making the zucchini fritters

Grate zucchinis, squeeze out excess liquid and place zucchinis in a bowl. Add ricotta and flour, and stir to combine. Add eggs and stir well to combine. Season with salt and pepper. Shape into 6 x 10cm rounds, then set aside.

4 Cooking the fritters

Preheat oven to 160C. Line 2 oven trays with paper towel. Heat 2cm oil in a large, deep frying pan over medium–high heat. Shallow-fry potato fritters for 2 minutes each side or until golden and cooked through, then place on prepared tray and transfer to the oven to keep warm (get an adult to help you). Repeat with the carrot and zucchini fritters. Place one of each fritter on plates and serve with mixed-leaf salad, aïoli and cucumber raita.

Chef's Tip

Cucumber raita is a classic Indian accompaniment for vegetable fritters. Combine 1 peeled, seeded, chopped Lebanese cucumber, 280g (1 cup) Greek-style yoghurt and ½ tsp ground cumin in a bowl, season with salt and pepper and stir to combine.

MY SCORE   /10

Haloumi is a Greek/Cypriot sheep's milk cheese. It is available from supermarkets and delis.

Roasted mushrooms & tomatoes with chargrilled haloumi

SERVES: 4
PREPARATION: 10 MINS
COOKING: 20 MINS

4 large (150g each)
   flat mushrooms,
   stalks trimmed
275g small truss
   tomatoes, cut into
   4 bunches
12 cloves garlic,
   unpeeled
80ml (⅓ cup) extra
   virgin olive oil
2 tbs olive oil, to brush
1 bunch asparagus,
   trimmed, halved (see
   Lesson #8, page 57)
100g baby spinach
250g haloumi, halved
   horizontally, then
   halved again to make
   4 pieces
Lemon wedges and
   toasted ciabatta
   (see recipe) to serve

1 Roasting mushrooms and tomatoes

Preheat oven to 200C. Place mushrooms, stalk-side up, on one side of a large ovenproof dish. Add tomatoes to the other side. Scatter with garlic, drizzle with 2 tbs extra virgin olive oil and season with salt and pepper. Roast for 20 minutes or until mushrooms are tender.

2 Cooking the vegetables

Five minutes before the mushrooms are cooked, heat 1 tbs olive oil in a non-stick frying pan. Add asparagus and cook, turning, for 2 minutes or until tender. Add spinach and cook for 30 seconds or until just wilted. Season, then set aside.

3 Cooking the haloumi

Brush a chargrill pan with remaining 1 tbs oil (or use same pan as asparagus and spinach) and heat over high heat. Add haloumi and cook for 2 minutes or until lightly charred underneath. Turn and cook for a further minute.

4 Assembling the dish

Squeeze garlic cloves from skins, then tear cloves into smaller pieces. Place 1 piece of haloumi on a plate, top with a mushroom and one-quarter each of the asparagus, spinach, and garlic and 1 bunch tomatoes. Season with salt and pepper. Repeat with remaining ingredients. Serve with lemon wedges and toasted ciabatta.

TOASTED CIABATTA

* Ciabatta is an Italian crusty white bread with a long, flat shape. Brush 8 thin slices of ciabatta on both sides with a little olive oil, season with salt and pepper, then chargrill for 45 seconds each side or until toasted.

Spinach and ricotta gnocchi

SERVES: 4
PREPARATION: 25 MINS
COOKING: 20 MINS

400g fresh firm ricotta*
2 x 250g pkts frozen
    spinach, defrosted,
    squeezed dry
2 tsp finely chopped
    oregano
1 lemon, zested
40g (½ cup) finely
    grated parmesan
60g (½ cup) finely
    grated gruyère (see
    Top Tip, page 23)
2 eggs, lightly beaten
105g (¾ cup) plain flour
Small basil leaves and
    shaved parmesan,
    to serve

Tomato sauce

1 tbs olive oil
1 onion, finely chopped
1 clove garlic, crushed
250ml (1 cup) chicken
    or vegetable stock
750ml (3 cups)
    passata (sieved
    puréed tomatoes)
1 tsp caster sugar
2 tbs chopped
    basil leaves

1 **Making the tomato sauce**
To make tomato sauce, heat oil in a deep frying pan over medium–high heat. Add onion and cook for 3 minutes or until soft. Add garlic and cook for 30 seconds. Add stock and passata, and stir to combine. Reduce heat to low and simmer for 10 minutes or until sauce thickens. Stir in sugar and chopped basil. Season with salt and pepper.

2 **Making the gnocchi**
To make gnocchi, place ricotta, spinach, oregano, lemon zest, cheeses, eggs and 75g (½ cup) flour in a large bowl. Season with salt and pepper, and stir to combine. Roll tablespoons of mixture into balls. Place remaining 30g flour in a bowl, then dust gnocchi in flour, shaking off excess.

3 **Cooking the gnocchi**
Bring a large saucepan of salted water to the boil. Cook gnocchi for 4 minutes or until they float to the surface. Remove gnocchi with a slotted spoon (get an adult to help you) and divide among bowls.

4 **Serving the gnocchi**
Divide gnocchi among bowls and spoon over tomato sauce. Season with salt and pepper. Scatter with basil leaves and shaved parmesan to serve.

Chef's Tip
To make mini gnocchi, use 2 tsp of mixture and cook for 2 minutes or until they float.

TOP TIPS
* Fresh firm ricotta is available from selected supermarkets and delis.
* For a smoother textured spinach mixture, process the mixture in a food processor.

In Italian, gnocchi means 'lumps' and probably comes from the word for the knot you find in a piece of wood, or perhaps from the Italian word for knuckle, 'nocca'.

MY SCORE   /10

about
SeaFooD

LESSON 9
Preparing prawns

1 To peel prawns, first remove the head by twisting it gently away from the body. Peel the shells with the legs (pull these away along the underside of the prawn). If you are also removing the tail, squeeze it and gently pull it away from the body. To butterfly prawns, using a sharp knife, score down the back of the prawn, as you would when removing the digestive tract (see right), cutting a little deeper, but not all the way through, so that the prawn can be opened up flat.

2 To remove the digestive tract, using a sharp knife, score down the back of the prawn to expose the dark 'vein' (this process is frequently described in recipes as 'deveining'). To remove the digestive tract without cutting along the back of the prawn, carefully pull out the vein through the opening at the top of the body where it joins the head.

When buying whole fish, look for plump, firm flesh and clear, shiny eyes. Fillets should also be shiny and firm to the touch. Fresh fish should smell of the sea; not too fishy!

LESSON 10
Pin-boning salmon

To pin-bone salmon, take a pair of fish tweezers (Regular tweezers work well, too, but make sure you wash them well before and after using them!!) and run your fingers over the fish to check for bones. If you find any, pull them out with the tweezers. Special fish tweezers are available from kitchenware shops.

Prawn laksa

SERVES: 4
PREPARATION: 15 MINS
COOKING: 5 MINS

200g rice vermicelli
  noodles*
1 tbs vegetable oil
60g sachet (¼ cup)
  laksa paste
750ml (3 cups)
  chicken stock
400ml can coconut milk
4 kaffir lime leaves (see
  Top Tips, page 89)
500g large green
  prawns, peeled,
  cleaned, leaving
  tails intact (see Lesson
  #9, page 69)
150g snow peas,
  trimmed, halved
  diagonally
1 tbs grated palm sugar
  or brown sugar (see
  Top Tips, page 89)
2 tbs fish sauce (see Top
  Tips, page 89)
½ cup coriander leaves
50g bean sprouts
Extra coriander sprigs,
  and lime wedges,
  to serve

1 Preparing the noodles

Place noodles in a heatproof bowl and pour over enough boiling water to cover. Stand for 5 minutes, then drain.

2 Cooking the prawns

Heat a wok over high heat, add oil and gently swirl to coat wok. Add laksa paste and cook for 1 minute or until fragrant. Add stock, coconut milk, kaffir lime leaves, prawns and snow peas. Bring to a simmer and cook for 3 minutes or until prawns change colour.

3 Serving the prawn laksa

Stir in sugar, fish sauce and coriander. Adjust seasoning, if necessary (the flavour should be a balance of sweet, salty and sour). To serve, divide noodles among 4 deep soup bowls and ladle soup over the top. Top with bean sprouts and extra coriander and serve with lime wedges.

Chef's Tip It is important to add the seasonings (palm sugar and fish sauce) at the very end to retain their flavour. To retain its zing, the lime juice is best squeezed over just before eating.

TOP TIP

* Rice vermicelli noodles are available from Asian grocers and the Asian section of selected supermarkets. They're also used in Asian noodle salads.

MY SCORE   /10

MY SCORE /10

Salmon with wasabi butter and Asian slaw

SERVES: 4
PREPARATION: 20 MINS
COOKING: 6 MINS

1 tbs vegetable oil
4 x 220g salmon fillets, skinned, pin-boned (see Lesson #10, page 69 and Chef's Tip)

Wasabi butter
100g butter, softened
2 cloves garlic, crushed
1 tsp wasabi paste*
1 tsp soy sauce
½ tsp finely grated ginger
1 tbs finely chopped coriander

Asian slaw
75g (¼ cup) mayonnaise
2 tsp soy sauce
2 tbs sesame seeds, toasted
80g (1 cup) finely shredded red cabbage
2 cups (100g) finely shredded wombok (Chinese cabbage)
4 eschalots, thinly sliced
3 tsp finely shredded pickled ginger*

1 Making the wasabi butter
To make wasabi butter, place all the ingredients in a bowl and stir to combine. Place butter mixture in a 5cm line on a piece of baking paper, roll up to enclose and twist ends to form a compact sausage shape. Refrigerate until firm. To serve, unwrap and slice butter into rounds.

2 Making the Asian slaw
Place mayonnaise, soy sauce and sesame seeds in a large bowl and stir to combine. Add cabbages, eschalots and ginger, and, using clean hands, toss well to combine.

3 Cooking the salmon
Heat oil in a large frying pan over medium–high heat. Cook salmon for 3 minutes each side or until just cooked through. Divide Asian slaw among bowls or plates, top each with a piece of salmon and serve with a round of wasabi butter.

Chef's Tip Try flaking the salmon after cooking and tossing through the slaw for an easy picnic idea.

TOP TIP
* Wasabi paste and shredded pickled ginger are available from Asian grocers and the Asian section of selected supermarkets.

Snapper fillets with caponata sauce

SERVES: 4
PREPARATION: 15 MINS
COOKING: 40 MINS

1 tbs olive oil
4 x 200g pieces
   snapper fillet, skin on
   pin-boned (see
   Lesson #10, page 69)
Steamed green beans
   (optional), to serve

Caponata sauce

500g vine-ripened
   tomatoes
100ml olive oil
350g eggplant, cut
   into 1cm cubes
1 red onion,
   finely chopped
2 clove garlic, crushed
2 stalks celery,
   finely chopped
45g (¼ cup) baby capers
1 sprig oregano
80g (½ cup) Sicilian
   olives, flesh sliced
   from pits, chopped
3 tsp caster sugar
80ml (⅓ cup) red
   wine vinegar
1 tbs chopped oregano

1 Peeling tomatoes for the caponata sauce

Using a small, sharp knife, cut a cross into the skin on the base of each tomato. Bring a saucepan of water to the boil. Add tomatoes to water and blanch for 1 minute or until skins start to peel away. Using a slotted spoon, remove tomatoes from pan and place in a bowl of iced water. Cool. Peel skins and discard, then cut flesh into 1cm pieces.

2 Making the caponata sauce

Heat 80ml (⅓ cup) oil in a large frying pan over high heat. Add eggplant and cook, stirring frequently, for 5 minutes or until softened. Remove from pan and set aside. Heat remaining 1 tbs oil in the same pan over medium–high heat. Cook onion, garlic and celery for 3 minutes or until soft. Reduce heat to low, add tomatoes, eggplant, capers, oregano sprig, olives, sugar and vinegar, and simmer, stirring occasionally, for 20 minutes or until vegetables are very tender. Stir in chopped oregano and season with salt and pepper.

3 Cooking the snapper fillets

Meanwhile, heat 1 tbs olive oil in a large frying pan over medium–high heat. Cook fish, skin-side down first, for 4 minutes, then turn over and cook for a further 4 minutes (depending on the thickness) or until just cooked. Divide fish among plates, top with caponata sauce and serve with steamed green beans, if using.

TOP TIP
* The flesh of Sicilian green olives is more difficult to remove than other olives because it's attached so tightly to the pit. Using a small knife, cut cheeks from the olive, rotating, until all flesh is removed.

MY SCORE   /10

The fish is so moist, with
a crunch on the outside, and
that tartare sauce is to
die for, my friend.
MATT MORAN
MY SCORE   /10

Marcus
Fish goujons with chips & tartare sauce

SERVES: 4
PREPARATION: 30 MINS
COOKING: 20 MINS
Goujon is the name used to describe any sort of crumbed or floured strip of fish.

1kg sebago potatoes, peeled, cut into fat chips, soaked in water
Peanut oil, to deep-fry
1 quantity tartare sauce (see Staples, page 4)
2 tsp chopped dill
Chopped flat-leaf parsley and lemon wedges, to serve

Fish goujons
150g (1 cup) self-raising flour
3 egg whites, lightly beaten
100g (1 cup) dried breadcrumbs
4 x 150g skinless perch or blue-eye trevalla fillets, halved lengthwise
80ml (⅓ cup) peanut oil

1 Preheat oven to 170C. To make chips, line an oven tray with several layers of paper towel. Fill a saucepan or deep-fryer one-third full with oil. Heat over medium heat until oil registers 180C on a thermometer (or see Top Tip). Drain potatoes and pat dry with paper towel (wet potatoes will make the oil spit). Fry chips, in 3 batches, for 4 minutes or until tender and pale golden (get an adult to help). Drain on lined tray, sprinkle with salt, then transfer to the oven to keep warm as you fry each batch.

2 For fish goujons, place flour and egg whites in separate bowls and place breadcrumbs on a plate. Dust each fish piece with flour, shaking off excess flour. Dip into egg white, then coat in breadcrumbs. Heat oil in a large frying pan over medium heat. Cook fish, in 2 batches, for 2 minutes each side or until golden and just cooked through. Drain on paper towel. Keep warm in oven.

3 Place tartare sauce in a small bowl and stir in dill. Divide fish goujons among plates, scatter with parsley and serve with chips, tartare sauce and lemon wedges.

ABOUT MARCUS
Marcus is 11 years old and lives in New South Wales. He got hooked on cooking when he watched the first series of *Junior MasterChef* (although he admits to not liking cleaning up!). This skateboarding fan won his stripes (and an apron) in the healthy fast-food challenge with this clever take on fish and chips.

TOP TIP
To test if oil is the right temperature, add a 1.5cm cube of bread to the pan. It should turn golden in 35 seconds.

ABOUT STEVEN

Twelve-year-old Steven hails from South Australia and, with his Greek and Italian heritage, loves cooking pizza and pasta. He'd never cooked a curry before, but went on to win the perfect curry challenge with this fantastic dish, impressing Gary and George, as well as guest judge, chef Kumar Mahadevan.

Steven
Golden seafood curry

SERVES: 4
PREPARATION: 35 MINS
COOKING: 20 MINS

1 large (300g) desiree potato, peeled, cut into 3cm pieces
400ml can coconut milk
125ml (½ cup) fish stock
500g firm white skinless fish fillets, cut into 3cm pieces
1 tbs fish sauce
2 tsp lime juice
1 tbs grated palm sugar
1 spring onion, sliced
Steamed jasmine rice, to serve

Yellow curry paste

1 tsp ground cumin
1 tsp ground coriander
½ tsp ground cinnamon
2 long red chillies, chopped, plus extra, thinly sliced, to serve
½ tsp ground turmeric
1 tsp grated ginger
2 cloves garlic, crushed
1 onion, chopped
1 stalk lemongrass (white part only), finely chopped
1 tbs roughly chopped coriander, plus extra leaves, to serve
1 tbs peanut oil
1 tbs fish sauce

1 To make yellow curry paste, place cumin, coriander and cinnamon in a small frying pan over medium heat and stir for 1 minute or until fragrant. Transfer to a small food processor or stick blender with remaining indredients and process to a paste.

2 To make curry, cook potato in a saucepan of boiling salted water for 5 minutes or until just tender. Drain and refresh under cold running water.

3 Place 200ml coconut milk in a large wok or deep frying pan and bring to the boil. Cook for 4 minutes or until coconut milk starts to separate and looks oily. Reduce heat to medium. Add curry paste and cook, stirring, for 4 minutes or until fragrant.

4 Add remaining coconut milk, fish stock, fish and potato, stir gently and cook for 3 minutes or until fish is just cooked. Stir in fish sauce, lime juice and palm sugar.

5 Spoon curry into a large bowl and scatter with spring onion and extra coriander leaves and chilli. Serve with steamed jasmine rice.

That is a great curry!
KUMAR MAHADEVAN
MY SCORE   /10

You really understand the balance of flavours. Well done!
ANNA GARE

MY SCORE   /10

Greta

Baked salmon with baby bok choy, tofu & asparagus

SERVES: 4
PREPARATION: 30 MINS
COOKING: 25 MINS

300g firm silken tofu
4 x 200g pieces salmon,
   skinned, pin-boned
   (see Lesson #10,
   page 69)
80ml (⅓ cup) olive oil
2 baby bok choy,
   quartered lengthwise
2 bunches asparagus,
   trimmed
2 tbs plain flour
2 cloves garlic,
   thickly sliced
Steamed rice, to serve

Marinade

60ml (¼ cup) red
   wine vinegar
1 tbs soy sauce
3 tsp caster sugar
2 cloves garlic, crushed
1 tbs olive oil
50g butter, melted

1 Preheat oven to 200C. Carefully place tofu on a chopping board. Cut into 12 equal cubes.

2 To make marinade, whisk all ingredients together and season with pepper. Place salmon in a glass or plastic dish, pour over marinade and set aside for 5 minutes.

3 Heat a large, non-stick frying pan over high heat. Add 1 tbs oil and cook salmon for 1 minute each side or until browned. Transfer to a plate. Tear 4 x 30cm x 40cm sheets of baking paper. Place one bok choy quarter and one-quarter of the asparagus in centre of baking paper. Top with salmon, then spoon over one-quarter of the marinade. Bring ends of paper up and over ingredients and fold together to secure. Repeat with remaining 3 pieces of baking paper, bok choy, asparagus, salmon and marinade. Place fish parcels on an oven tray. Bake for 7 minutes or until just cooked. Set aside to rest.

4 Meanwhile, place a large frying pan over medium–high heat and add 2 tbs oil. Combine flour with 1 tsp salt and ½ tsp pepper. Coat half of the tofu in seasoned flour and fry for 6 minutes, turning, or until golden. Repeat with the remaining tofu.

5 Place garlic and remaining 1 tbs olive oil in a small frying pan. Cook, stirring, over medium heat, for 2 minutes or until golden. Reserve oil.

6 To serve, transfer paper parcels to plates, then open (be careful of the steam). Top with crisp garlic and reserved oil, then scatter with tofu. Serve with steamed rice.

ABOUT GRETA

Greta is 11 years old and from West Australia. She's been cooking for a few years – even trying her hand at chef Peter Gilmore's snow egg. Her talent stood her in good stead for the conveyor belt mystery box challenge – she won it with this salmon dish.

ABOUT ZAC

Twelve-year-old Zac lives in New South Wales, and says he started cooking because his mum isn't that good! While he enjoys cooking family meals, he also loves being creative. He proved as much when he came third in the Asian invention test, winning the heart of guest judge Luke Nguyen in the process.

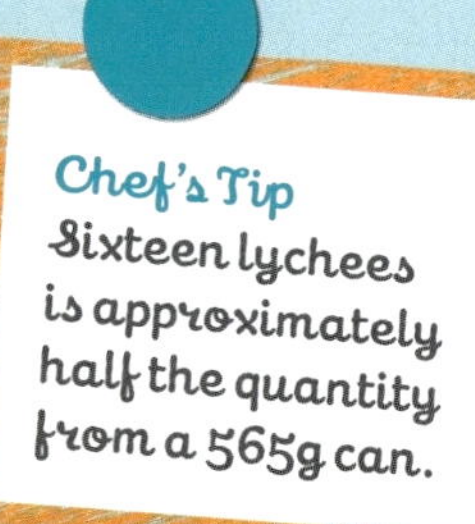

Chef's Tip
Sixteen lychees is approximately half the quantity from a 565g can.

Zac
Thai prawn salad with red nam jim

SERVES: 4
PREPARATION: 35 MINS
COOKING: 5 MINS

Red nam jim is a Thai dressing with spicy, salty, sweet and sour flavours.

20 large green prawns
750ml (3 cups) fish stock
1 cup coriander leaves
1 cup mint leaves
1 cup Thai basil leaves
½ cup Vietnamese mint leaves*
16 canned lychees (see Chef's Tip)
6 red eschalots, peeled, thinly sliced
80g unsalted roasted peanuts, roughly chopped
1 telegraph cucumber, halved lengthwise, seeded, thinly sliced
8 kaffir lime leaves, thinly shredded

Red nam jim
2 cloves garlic
3cm piece ginger, peeled, finely grated
2 coriander roots
1 long red chilli, thinly sliced
1 tbs grated palm sugar
1 tbs lime juice
3 tsp fish sauce

1 Peel, clean and butterfly the prawns, leaving tails intact (see Lesson #9, page 69). Place fish stock in a saucepan and bring to a simmer over medium heat. Add prawns and cook for 2 minutes or until they change colour and are just cooked through. Drain prawns and set aside. Discard stock.

2 To make red nam jim, using a mortar and pestle, pound garlic, ginger, coriander roots and chilli to a paste (take care not to touch your eyes, as chilli will sting). Add palm sugar, lime juice and fish sauce, checking the balance of sweet, salty and sour tastes, and remembering that the lychees will add sweetness to the salad. Makes ⅓ cup.

3 Place herbs, lychees, eschalots and peanuts in a large bowl. Add cucumber to salad with prawns and red nam jim. Toss gently to combine, then divide among plates and scatter with kaffir lime leaves to serve.

TOP TIP
*Vietnamese mint is from selected greengrocers and Asian grocers. If unavailable, increase the quantity of the other herbs.

I think your presentation
is fantastic, and you really
nailed that dressing.
LUKE NGUYEN

MY SCORE   /10

about
MEAT

LESSON 11
Pounding chicken breasts

1 Remove the chicken tenderloin (the long, thin strip attached to the underside of the breast) and reserve it for another use.

2 Place the chicken breast between two sheets of plastic wrap and, using the flat side of a meat mallet or a rolling pin, pound until 5mm thick. This technique can also be used for pork, veal and beef in recipes that require the meat to be cooked quickly and evenly, such as schnitzels.

LESSON 12
Butterflying spatchcock

1 Using poultry shears or kitchen scissors, cut the spatchcock along each side of the backbone (pictured far left), then remove and discard the backbone.

2 Turn the spatchcock over, breast-side up. Using the heel of your hand, press down firmly on the breastbone of the spatchcock to flatten it.

LESSON 13
Testing steaks

Cook a 2cm-thick piece of steak for 2 minutes on each side for rare, 4 minutes for medium and 6 minutes for well done. To test if your steak is done, press the centre with the back of the tongs. The steak will feel soft when it's rare, slightly firmer and springy when it's medium and very firm when it's well done. Transfer steak to a plate, cover loosely with foil and set aside for 5–10 minutes to rest. This allows the juices and muscle fibres to settle, ensuring the steak is tender.

Mini shepherd's pies

SERVES: 4
PREPARATION: 20 MINS
COOKING: 1 HR 5 MINS

1 tbs olive oil
1 onion, finely chopped
2 cloves garlic, crushed
1 carrot, cut into
   5mm pieces
1 stalk celery,
   finely chopped
750g minced lamb
1½ tbs plain flour
250ml (1 cup) beef stock
1 sprig rosemary
   or thyme
2 bay leaves
2 tsp Worcestershire
   sauce
1 tbs tomato paste
750g desiree potatoes,*
   peeled, chopped
45g butter, chopped
125ml (½ cup) milk

1 Cooking the onion
Heat oil in a large, deep frying pan over medium–high heat. Add onion and cook, stirring, for 3 minutes or until slightly softened. Add garlic, carrot and celery. Reduce heat to low–medium and cook, stirring frequently, for 5 minutes or until softened.

2 Cooking the mince
Increase heat to high and add mince. Cook for 5 minutes or until lightly browned, breaking up any lumps with a wooden spoon. Add flour and stir for 1 minute. Add stock, rosemary, bay leaves, Worcestershire sauce and tomato paste, and stir to combine. Bring to the boil, then reduce heat to low and simmer, stirring occasionally, for 30 minutes or until mixture has reduced and thickened.

3 Cooking the potatoes
Meanwhile, preheat oven to 180C. Place potatoes in a large saucepan of cold water. Bring to the boil over medium–high heat and cook for 15 minutes or until tender. Drain, then return potatoes to pan. Add 30g chopped butter and, using a potato masher, mash until smooth. Add milk and stir to combine. Season with salt and pepper.

4 Baking the shepherd's pies
Divide mince mixture among 4 x 500ml (2-cup) ovenproof dishes. Spoon mash over lamb mixture to cover, then using a fork, fluff mash to roughen the surface. Place remaining 15g butter in a microwave-safe bowl and microwave on low for 15 seconds to melt. Brush mashed potato with melted butter. Place dishes on an oven tray and bake for 20 minutes or until tops are golden. Serve immediately.

TOP TIP
* When buying potatoes, choose ones that are similar in size so they can be cut and cooked evenly. If you peel potatoes ahead of time, submerge them fully in a bowl of cold water to prevent them from going brown.

MY SCORE   /10

MY SCORE   /10

Thai beef salad

SERVES: 4
PREPARATION: 20 MINS
COOKING: 6 MINS

1 tbs vegetable oil
500g rump steaks
1 Lebanese cucumber
4 spring onions
50g mixed baby lettuce
  leaves (mesclun)
½ cup mint leaves, torn
½ cup coriander leave
2 kaffir lime leaves,*
  finely shredded
200g cherry tomatoes,
  halved

Dressing
1 stalk lemongrass*
  (white part only),
  finely chopped
60ml (¼ cup) lime juice
2 tbs fish sauce*
1 tbs grated palm sugar*

1 Cooking the steaks
Heat oil in a frying pan over medium–high heat. Add steaks and cook for 3 minutes each side for medium-rare, or until cooked to your liking (see Lesson #13, page 85). Transfer to a plate and rest for 10 minutes.

2 Making the dressing
Meanwhile, place all ingredients in a small bowl and whisk gently until sugar dissolves.

3 Assembling the salad
Halve cucumber lengthwise, then slice thinly on the diagonal and place in a large bowl. Trim ends of spring onions, slice thinly on the diagonal, then add to the cucumber with lettuce, mint, coriander, kaffir lime leaves and tomatoes. Thinly slice beef across the grain, then add to salad. Pour dressing over beef mixture and toss to combine. Serve Thai beef salad immediately.

> Meat has lines that look a little like wood grain running through it. These are known as 'the grain' of the meat. Slicing across, rather than along, the grain enhances tenderness.

TOP TIPS

Pictured, from left to right
* Kaffir lime leaves add a citrus tang to dishes. Substitute with the finely grated zest of 1 lime.
* Fish sauce adds a salty element to Asian dishes. It is made from fermented fish or shellfish.
* Lemongrass has a sharp citrus scent and flavour. Use only the white part for cooking. The grassy leaves are used to make a refreshing tea.
* Palm sugar is made by boiling the sap of palm trees. It varies in colour from almost black to creamy gold. It's sold in blocks, then grated for cooking. Substitute brown sugar. All are available from selected supermarkets and Asian grocers.

Chicken pot pies

SERVES: 4
PREPARATION: 25 MINS
COOKING: 1 HR 10 MINS

1 tbs olive oil
1.5kg chicken
  'lovely legs'*
750ml (3 cups)
  chicken stock
2 sprigs thyme
2 bay leaves
60g butter, chopped
1 large leek,*
  (white part only)
  quartered lengthwise,
  thinly sliced
2 cloves garlic, crushed
250g button
  mushrooms, quartered
35g (¼ cup) plain flour
120g (1 cup) frozen peas
1 or 2 sheets frozen puff
  pastry (see Chef's Tip)
1 egg, lightly beaten
Green salad, to serve

1 Cooking the chicken
Heat oil in a large, deep frying pan over high heat. Add chicken and cook for 1 minute each side or until browned. Add stock, thyme and bay leaves. Reduce heat to low, cover with a lid and simmer for 30 minutes or until meat is starting to fall off the bones. Using tongs, transfer chicken to a bowl. Cool. Strain stock and reserve. Discard herbs.

2 Chopping the chicken
Pull meat from bones and discard bones. Roughly chop chicken into 2cm pieces.

3 Cooking the chicken mixture
Preheat oven to 200C. Heat butter in a deep frying pan over low–medium heat. Add leek and cook, stirring occasionally, for 5 minutes or until softened. Add garlic and mushrooms, and cook for 5 minutes or until vegetables are soft. Add flour and cook, stirring, for 1 minute or until well combined. Gradually add reserved stock. Stir in chicken and peas, and simmer for 5 minutes or until the sauce thickens.

4 Baking the pies
Divide chicken mixture among 4 x 500ml (2-cup) ovenproof dishes. Cut pastry into 4 squares large enough to cover tops of dishes. Place over filling. Lightly brush pastry with egg. Using the tip of a small, sharp knife, cut 2 x 1cm slits into the pastry to allow steam to escape. Bake for 20 minutes or until puffed and golden. Serve pies immediately with green salad.

Chef's Tip
Depending on the diameter of your dishes, you may need to use 2 puff pastry sheets, cut in half, to cover them.

TOP TIPS
* Chicken 'lovely legs' are skinless chicken legs available from supermarkets.
* Leeks contain a lot of grit, so after cutting, rinse them under cold running water or in a bowl of water to remove any grit.

MY SCORE /10

Your roast chicken
is right up there!
GEORGE CALOMBARIS

MY SCORE   /10

Alysha
Roast balsamic chicken & champ

SERVES: 4
PREPARATION: 1 HR
COOKING: 1 HR 10 MINS
Champ is a traditional Irish mashed potato dish.

3 capsicums (yellow, red and green), seeded, cut into 1.5cm strips
1 red onion, cut into thin wedges
8 cloves garlic, unpeeled
6 sprigs thyme
100ml olive oil
4 x chicken marylands, at room temperature
125ml (½ cup) balsamic vinegar
1 tbs brown sugar
250g cherry tomatoes

Champ
800g desiree potatoes, peeled, cut into 3cm pieces
4 cloves garlic, unpeeled
120g (½ cup) sour cream
60g butter, chopped
3 spring onions, thinly sliced
2 tbs milk

1 Preheat oven to 200C. Combine capsicums, onion, garlic, thyme and 1 tbs oil in a large roasting pan. Place chicken on top. Whisk vinegar, 80ml (⅓ cup) oil and sugar in a bowl until combined. Season with salt and pepper. Drizzle half the marinade over chicken, then season. Roast for 40 minutes or until chicken is cooked through (see Chef's Tip). Transfer to a plate and cover loosely with foil. Reserve 125ml (½ cup) of cooking juices from the pan in a bowl. Add tomatoes to pan and roast for a further 12 minutes or until vegetables are tender.

2 Meanwhile, to make champ, bring a large saucepan of salted water to the boil over high heat. Add potatoes and garlic, reduce heat to medium and simmer for 12 minutes or until potatoes are tender. Drain and reserve garlic. Return potatoes to pan. Stir over low heat for 2 minutes or until dry. Mash potatoes until almost smooth. Peel garlic, mash with a fork, then add to potatoes. Add sour cream, spring onions and milk, and stir to combine.

3 Pour remaining half of marinade into a saucepan with reserved cooking juices. Cook over medium heat, stirring frequently, for 5 minutes or until sauce thickens slightly.

4 Divide chicken, vegetables and herbs among plates and drizzle over sauce. Serve with champ.

ABOUT ALYSHA
West Australian Alysha is 12 years old and already has a couple of careers in mind – a chef or a singer. We're hoping it's the former, because a dish like this, which won her the perfect roast challenge, is just that – a winner!

Chef's Tip To test if chicken is cooked through, insert a skewer into the thickest part of the thigh. If the juices run clear, the chicken is done. If not, cook for a further 5 minutes and test again.

Harry
Pan-fried duck breast with Thai herb & cucumber salad

SERVES: 4
PREPARATION: 25 MINS
COOKING: 10 MINS

1 bunch coriander
2 x 250g duck breasts
1 telegraph cucumber,
   halved lengthwise,
   seeded, cut on
   the diagonal
1 cup mint leaves
½ cup Thai basil leaves
3 spring onions,
   thinly sliced
1 long red chilli,
   thinly sliced
60g (½ cup) roasted
   unsalted peanuts,
   coarsely chopped

Dressing
1 stalk lemongrass
   (white part only),
   finely chopped
2 tbs lime juice
1 tbs fish sauce
2 tbs grated palm sugar
1 tsp sesame oil

ABOUT HARRY

Eleven-year-old Harry comes from West Australia and was taught to cook by his grandmother. He loves to experiment – just like another person who inspires him, British chef Heston Blumenthal. Harry thrives on the creativity of the invention tests and this impressive dish is a perfect example of that.

1 Pick coriander leaves from bunch and measure 1 cup leaves. Trim roots with 3cm stem, wash well, then finely chop and reserve for dressing.

2 Using a sharp knife, score the skin of the duck breasts every 5mm, being careful not to cut into the flesh. Season with salt and pepper. Place, skin-side down, in an unheated non-stick frying pan. Place frying pan over medium–high heat and cook for 6 minutes or until skin is deep golden. Turn and cook for a further 4 minutes or until medium-rare. (Duck meat tastes better if it's a little pink in the centre; however, cook it for longer if you prefer it well done.)

3 To make dressing, using a mortar and pestle, pound reserved chopped coriander roots and lemongrass to a coarse paste. Add lime juice, fish sauce, palm sugar and sesame oil, and stir to combine. Alternatively, purée all dressing ingredients in a blender.

4 Place cucumber, 1 cup coriander leaves, mint, Thai basil, spring onions and chilli in a large bowl. Add dressing and toss gently to combine. Slice duck, add to salad and scatter with chopped peanuts to serve.

The duck is perfectly cooked
and I love that dressing
– it has beautiful balance.
MATT MORAN

MY SCORE   /10

The balance of flavours
is beyond your years.
Clever cooking!
GEORGE CALOMBARIS

MY SCORE   /10

Madi
Hera's lamb

SERVES: 4
PREPARATION: 25 MINS
COOKING: 40 MINS

2 x 250g lamb
   backstraps
25g (¼ cup) walnuts,
   finely chopped
40g (¼ cup) pitted
   Sicilian green olives
   (see Top Tip, page 74),
   finely chopped
1 small eschalot, peeled,
   finely chopped
2 tbs Craisins (sweetened
   dried cranberries)
2 tsp finely chopped
   flat-leaf parsley
1 tbs walnut oil
2 tsp pomegranate
   molasses (see
   Chef's Tip)
½ lemon, zested, plus
   2 tsp lemon juice
1 tbs olive oil
4 fresh figs, cross-cut
   two-thirds of the way
   through
Warmed honey, to drizzle

Lemon, garlic & feta potatoes

400g chat potatoes,
   quartered lengthwise
2 tsp chopped rosemary
2 tsp lemon juice
1 clove garlic, crushed
2 tbs olive oil
50g (¼ cup) Greek feta,
   crumbled

1 Preheat oven to 200C. To make potatoes, cook in a saucepan of boiling salted water for 5 minutes or until slightly soft. Drain potatoes and place in an ovenproof dish. Combine rosemary, lemon juice, garlic and oil, pour over potatoes and toss gently to combine. Roast for 25 minutes, turning halfway, or until tender.

2 Meanwhile, to make lamb, cut two-thirds of the way through the length of each backstrap along the centre to make a pocket. Combine walnuts in a bowl with olives, eschalot, Craisins, parsley, walnut oil, pomegranate molasses, lemon zest and juice. Season with salt and pepper. Fill pockets in lamb with stuffing, then tie lamb with kitchen string at 3cm intervals (or toothpicks) to secure.

3 Heat oil in a large frying pan. Add lamb and cook for 1 minute each side or until browned. Transfer to an oven tray and roast for 8 minutes for medium or until cooked to your liking. Loosely cover with foil and rest for 5 minutes.

4 Divide potatoes among plates and scatter over feta. Cut lamb into 2cm-thick slices and place over potatoes. Spoon any lamb cooking juices over. Place a fig on each plate and drizzle with honey to serve.

ABOUT MADI

Eleven-year-old Madi lives in New South Wales and enjoys making desserts and pastries. Another fan of chef Heston Blumenthal, she loves the fact that he pushes the boundaries with his cooking. This lamb dish, which won Madi the Greek challenge, is a fine example of this cook's kitchen smarts.

Chef's Tip

Pomegranate molasses is a tangy syrup made from pomegranate seeds, available from delis and Middle Eastern food shops. Substitute red wine vinegar.

Tom
Chicken marylands with baked fennel

SERVES: 4
PREPARATION: 20 MINS
COOKING: 30 MINS

1½ tbs chopped tarragon
1 tbs chopped rosemary
2 garlic gloves
1 tbs olive oil
4 chicken marylands

Baked fennel
50g butter, chopped,
   plus extra, to grease
2 small bulbs fennel
2 tsp plain flour
4 rindless bacon rashers,
   roughly chopped
60ml (¼ cup) double
   cream
60g (¾ cup) grated
   parmesan

Almond & mint sauce
40g (¼ cup) blanched
   almonds, roasted,
   finely chopped
⅓ cup chopped
   mint leaves
2 garlic cloves, crushed
1 tsp caster sugar
60ml (¼ cup)
   lemon juice
125ml (½ cup) olive oil

1 Preheat oven to 220C. Using a mortar and pestle, pound tarragon, rosemary, garlic and a pinch of salt to a paste. Add oil and stir to combine. Line a roasting pan with baking paper. Place chicken in pan and rub with paste. Roast for 30 minutes or until golden and cooked through.

2 Meanwhile, to make baked fennel, grease a 1L glass or ceramic baking dish with butter. Trim tough ends of fennel stems, leaving most of the stem. Discard outer layer and cut fennel into 1.5cm-thick slices. Cook in boiling salted water for 5 minutes or until tender. Drain. Pat dry with paper towel. Dust with flour.

3 Melt half the butter in a large frying pan over medium heat. Add fennel and cook for 1 minute each side or until golden. Transfer to prepared baking dish. Add bacon to same pan and cook, stirring, for 3 minutes or until golden, then scatter over fennel.

4 Add cream to pan and bring to the boil. Season with salt and pepper. Drizzle cream over fennel in baking dish. Sprinkle with parmesan and remaining 25g butter. Bake for 15 minutes or until parmesan is golden.

5 To make almond and mint sauce, combine all ingredients in a bowl. Season. To serve, divide chicken marylands and baked fennel among plates and drizzle with sauce.

ABOUT TOM
For someone whose specialty is lemon meringue pie, this 11-year-old from New South Wales sure can cook savoury dishes! This delicious roasted chicken he cooked in the perfect roast challenge saved Tom from elimination – and for good reason.

There's so much flavour in the chicken. One of the best dishes I've tasted today!
GARY MEHIGAN
MY SCORE /10

This is absolutely smashing
- really special.
I want the recipe!
GARY MEHIGAN
MY SCORE   /10

Indigo
Skordalia spatchcock

SERVES: 4
PREPARATION: 45 MINS
COOKING: 55 MINS

1½ tsp sweet paprika
1 tsp ground cumin
1 tsp ground cinnamon
¼ tsp freshly grated
  nutmeg
¼ cup each oregano,
  flat-leaf parsley and
  mint, chopped
1 tbs thyme leaves
½ red onion,
  finely chopped
125ml (½ cup)
  lemon juice
100ml extra virgin
  olive oil
4 x 500g spatchcocks
100g butter, chopped
300g green beans,
  trimmed
2 ripe tomatoes, cut
  into wedges
100g (½ cup) Greek feta
1 lemon, zested
Mint leaves, Greek-style
  yoghurt and lemon
  wedges, to serve

Skordalia

800g desiree potatoes
3 slices day-old bread,
  crusts removed
4 cloves garlic, peeled
1 tbs lemon juice
1 tbs white wine vinegar
80ml (⅓ cup) olive oil

1 Preheat oven to 200C. To make marinade, place 1 tsp paprika, cumin, cinnamon, nutmeg, 1 tsp salt and black pepper in a large bowl. Add herbs, onion and 80ml (⅓ cup) each of lemon juice and oil, and stir to combine.

2 Rinse spatchcocks and pat dry with paper towel. Butterfly and flatten spatchocks (see Lesson #12, page 85). Divide between 2 oven trays. Pour marinade over spatchocks on each tray and rub all over, then top with butter. Roast, swapping trays halfway, for 35 minutes or until cooked through.

3 Meanwhile, to make skordalia, peel and chop potatoes. Cook in a saucepan of boiling salted water for 12 minutes or until tender. Drain, then return to the pan. Stir over low heat for 2 minutes or until dry, then mash. Soak bread in a bowl of water for 1 minute, then squeeze dry. Process bread with garlic, lemon juice, vinegar and oil in a food processor until smooth. Add to mashed potatoes and stir to combine.

4 Cook beans in boiling salted water for 2 minutes or until tender. Drain, then refresh under cold running water. Whisk remaining 1 tbs olive oil and 2 tbs lemon juice in a bowl. Season. Add beans, tomatoes and feta, and toss gently to combine. Spread skordalia on each plate, top with a spatchcock and scatter with zest, mint and remaining ½ tsp paprika. Serve with bean salad, yoghurt and lemon wedges.

ABOUT INDIGO

Twelve-year-old Indigo hails from Queensland. She's a keen horsewoman and owns two horses. Her father was once a chef – he's passed on his love of cooking and skills to her. Indigo loves cooking rustic flavours, with ingredients from her vegetable garden. This dish, which was a standout in the Greek challenge, illustrates her cooking style perfectly.

Skordalia is a classic Greek sauce that's served with anything from fried fish to slow-roasted lamb.

about
dEsSErtS

To melt small quantities of chocolate, place a bowl over a pan of simmering water, then turn off the heat. The residual heat from the bowl will melt the chocolate.

LESSON 14
Rolling out pastry

1 Pastry is easier to work with if it's cold, so chill it for 30 minutes before rolling it and work quite quickly. If your pastry does become warm, return it to the fridge to firm up. Shape the piece of dough into roughly the shape you want. You can roll out pastry in two ways: lightly sprinkle a work surface with flour (this will help to stop the pastry sticking) and roll the pastry on the work surface; or roll it between 2 sheets of baking paper. Using a rolling pin, roll pastry from the centre outwards, turning pastry 45 degrees after each roll to keep an even shape. As pastry expands, press in edges with your hand and roll parallel to the edges to stop it cracking.

2 To transfer pastry to a baking pan, place the rolling pin across the pastry and loosely roll the pastry around it. Place it over the pan and slowly unroll it, so that it drops into the pan and overhangs the edge. Then, using your fingers, gently push the pastry into corners of the pan where the side meets the base. To trim the pastry with a rolling pin, roll the rolling pin lightly across the top of the pan; this will cut the excess pastry neatly. To trim with a knife, use the top of the pan as a guide as you trim. Chill the pastry for 20–30 minutes before baking to minimise shrinkage (or place in the freezer for 10 minutes).

LESSON 15
Melting chocolate

1 Place the chocolate in a glass or stainless-steel bowl. Pick a saucepan that the bowl will sit over snugly and fill the pan one-third full with water. Bring the water to a gentle simmer. Place the bowl over the pan (get an adult to help you), making sure it doesn't touch the simmering water, then stir occasionally until chocolate has melted.

This is absolutely amazing
- it tastes brilliant. High five!
GARY MEHIGAN
MY SCORE   /10

Chandler
Raspberry top tarts with white chocolate & mixed berries

SERVES: 4
PREPARATION: 45 MINS
COOKING: 35 MINS
Allow 1½ hrs for cooling, chilling and setting.

150g (12) savoiardi biscuits (Italian sponge finger biscuits, available from supermarkets)
100g unsalted butter, melted
250g cream cheese, softened, chopped
120g (½ cup) sour cream
1 egg
110g (½ cup) caster sugar
½ tsp vanilla extract
100g White Chocolate Melts
125g each raspberries and blueberries
Icing sugar, to dust

Raspberry coulis
300g frozen raspberries, thawed
55g (¼ cup) caster sugar

1 Preheat oven to 150C. Grease 4 x 12cm tart pans with removable bases.

2 Process biscuits in a food processor until mixture resembles crumbs. Add butter and process until combined. Divide mixture among tart pans. Using your fingers or the back of a teaspoon, press crumbs into bases and sides of pans. Chill for 15 minutes or until firm.

3 Meanwhile, to make coulis, place raspberries and sugar in saucepan over low heat and stir until sugar dissolves. Increase heat to medium and simmer for 8 minutes or until thickened slightly. Process mixture in a processor until smooth. Strain through a sieve over a bowl, pressing purée with the back of a spoon. Discard seeds.

4 Process cream cheese in a food processor until smooth. Add sour cream, egg, sugar and vanilla, and process until smooth. Divide mixture among tart pans.

5 Drizzle 1 tbs coulis over each tart, then, using a skewer, swirl the coulis lightly over the top to form a pattern. Place tarts on an oven tray and bake for 25 minutes or until set. Cool for 30 minutes, then refrigerate for 30 minutes or until set.

ABOUT CHANDLER
Chandler is 11 years old and comes from South Australia. He loves making desserts and has already started his own cooking business! He's a big fan of pâtissier Adriano Zumbo, who'd be well impressed with this winning recipe from the chocolate invention test.

6 Meanwhile, line an oven tray with baking paper. Place chocolate in a heatproof bowl and place over a saucepan of barely simmering water (don't allow bowl to touch water – see Lesson #15, page 103) and stir until melted. Pour into a zip-lock bag, seal, then, using scissors, snip a 5mm slit in one corner. Starting from the middle, pipe a spiral onto the tray, overlapping the circle slightly as the spiral widens. Repeat to make 4 spirals. Stand for 15 minutes or until set. To serve, spoon a little raspberry coulis onto plates, top with a tart, mixed berries and a white chocolate swirl. Dust with icing sugar.

Miraede
Flock of lambs

ABOUT MIRAEDE

Cheeky Miraede is 10 years old and comes from South Australia. While she wowed Matt Moran with her beef curry in the preliminary heats, she adores making desserts. And she prides herself on her presentation skills – such as these oh-so-cute cupcakes from the Mad Hatter challenge!

MAKES: 24
PREPARATION: 25 MINS
COOKING: 10 MINS

100g unsalted butter, softened
½ tsp vanilla extract
110g (½ cup) caster sugar
1 egg
150g (1 cup) self-raising flour, sifted
2 tbs milk
1 lemon, zested

Cupcake decoration
Ready-made white frosting*
100g pkt pink and white mini marshmallows, (use white only)
1 tube black decorating gel*

1 Preheat oven to 200C. Line 2 x 12-hole (2 tbs) mini cupcake pans with paper cases.

2 Using an electric mixer, beat butter, vanilla and sugar until pale and fluffy. Add egg and beat until combined. Add flour, milk and lemon zest, and beat until mixture is smooth.

3 Using a teaspoon, spoon cake batter into cupcake cases. Bake for 10 minutes or until risen (they should spring back when gently pressed). Transfer pans to a wire rack to cool.

4 To decorate, spread white frosting over cooled cupcakes. Press marshmallows into frosting, leaving a space on one side for the face. Using black decorating gel, apply dots and a mouth to create a face. Place cupcakes on a platter to serve.

TOP TIPS
* Ready-made white frosting and black decorating gel are from supermarkets.
* For a twist, stir the zest of a grated orange and 2 tsp poppyseeds into the cake batter for orange poppyseed cupcakes.

Spectacular presentation and your cupcakes are feather-light!
ANNA GARE
MILK
MY SCORE /10

The praline's fantastic,
and those tuiles – that
crunch is just what you
want. Well done!
MATT MORAN

MY SCORE   /10

Dee
Banana & praline parfait

SERVES: 10
PREPARATION: 20 MINS
COOKING: 20 MINS
Allow an extra 5 hours for freezing.

5 bananas
2 tsp lemon juice
2 egg whites
165g (¾ cup) caster sugar
300ml double cream

Praline
220g (1 cup) caster sugar
105g (¾ cup) roasted, peeled hazelnuts
Sunflower oil, to grease

Tuiles
1 egg white
55g (¼ cup) caster sugar
25g unsalted butter, melted
2 tbs plain flour
½ lemon, zested

1 Grease and line a 1.2L (13cm x 25cm) loaf pan with a strip of baking paper long enough to overhang sides. Mash 3 bananas together with 1 tsp lemon juice. Using an electric mixer, whisk egg whites with remaining 1 tsp lemon juice until stiff peaks form (see Lesson #4, page 29). Gradually add 110g (½ cup) sugar and whisk until thick and glossy.

2 Using a balloon whisk, whisk cream briefly until thickened. Gently fold cream into egg whites, followed by mashed bananas and half the crushed praline. Spoon into prepared loaf pan, level the top and freeze for at least 5 hours or overnight until firm.

3 To make praline, combine sugar and 80ml (⅓ cup) water in a heavy-based saucepan and stir over low heat until sugar dissolves. Brush down sides of pan with a pastry brush dipped in water to remove any sugar crystals. Increase heat to high and cook, without stirring, for 7 minutes or until a golden caramel. Remove from heat and immediately stir in nuts. Working quickly, pour mixture onto a lightly oiled oven tray. Spread with a palette knife and leave to cool. When praline is set, using a rolling pin, crush into large pieces, then place in a zip-lock bag, seal and finely crush with rolling pin.

4 Meanwhile, to make tuiles, preheat oven to 180C. Line 2 oven trays with baking paper. Using an electric mixer, beat egg white until frothy, add sugar and beat until well combined. Add butter, flour and lemon zest, and stir to combine. Spoon level teaspoonfuls of mixture onto prepared trays and spread thinly into 10cm-long strips. Bake for 5 minutes or until just beginning to colour on edges. Cool on trays.

5 Slice remaining 2 bananas and toss with remaining 55g (¼ cup) sugar in a bowl. Heat a large, non-stick frying pan over medium heat. Add bananas and cook, turning, for 1½ minutes or until caramelised. Slice parfait and serve on a plate with caramelised banana, a tuile and remaining praline.

ABOUT DEE
Twelve-year-old Dee is from New South Wales. He loves sailing and fishing. He considers himself quite adventurous with his cooking, and would like to be a head pastry chef one day. His recipe, from the ice-cream challenge early in the series, shows that he's well on his way to fulfilling that dream.

MY SCORE   /10

Pear frangipane tart

SERVES: **6**
PREPARATION: **25 MINS**
COOKING: **45 MINS**

825g can pear halves, drained, patted dry with paper towel
2 tsp caster sugar
1 tbs slivered almonds
2 tbs apricot jam
Double cream or vanilla ice-cream, to serve

Pastry

150g (1 cup) plain flour
75g unsalted butter, softened
1 egg yolk
2 tbs icing sugar

Frangipane filling

125g unsalted butter, softened
150g icing sugar, sifted
2 eggs
100g ground almonds
1 tbs plain flour

1 Making the pastry
Process flour and butter in a food processor until mixture resembles crumbs. Add egg yolk and icing sugar, and process until mixture just comes together. Turn out onto a lightly floured work surface and shape pastry into a disc. Wrap in plastic wrap and refrigerate for 30 minutes.

2 Preparing the tart case
Grease a 22cm tart pan with a removable base. Roll out pastry between 2 sheets of baking paper to a 30cm round. Carefully lift pastry into the pan to line the pan. Press pastry into the pan. Trim the edge with a rolling pin or knife (see Lesson #14, page 103). Refrigerate the tart case for 30 minutes.

3 Blind-baking the tart base
Preheat oven to 180C. Crumple up a sheet of baking paper, then smooth it out on the benchtop (this will allow it to sit more snugly in the tart case). Line the chilled tart case with the paper, then fill with dried beans or rice. Place tart case on an oven tray, then bake for 10 minutes. Remove paper and rice, and bake for a further 5 minutes or until pastry is light golden and dry. Cool.

4 Making the frangipane filling
Using an electric mixer, beat butter and icing sugar in a bowl until pale and fluffy. Add eggs, one at a time, beating well after each addition. Fold in ground almonds and flour. Spoon the mixture into the cooled tart case, then arrange pear halves, cut-side down, with round edges outwards, in a circle on top. Sprinkle with caster sugar and slivered almonds. Bake for 30 minutes or until the frangipane is puffed and golden.

5 Serving the tart
Place jam in a small microwave-safe glass bowl and microwave on low for 20 seconds or until runny. Brush warm jam over the top of the tart to glaze, then slice and serve with cream or vanilla ice-cream.

Frangipane is an almond-based paste or filling that also gives its name to the tart itself. Usually it's topped with fruit and slivered almonds, then glazed.

Chocolate & macadamia croissant puddings

SERVES: 6
PREPARATION: 10 MINS
COOKING: 30 MINS

Softened butter,
  to grease
6 large croissants
175g dark chocolate
  (70% cocoa solids),
  chopped
55g (¼ cup) caster sugar
4 eggs
1 tsp vanilla extract
300ml pouring cream
250ml (1 cup) milk
70g (½ cup)
  macadamias, chopped
Icing sugar, to dust
Double cream, to serve

1 Preparing the croissants

Preheat oven to 180C. Grease 6 x 250ml (1-cup) ramekins with soft butter. Cut croissants into 1.5cm slices and divide among ramekins, arranging them in a spiral pattern. Tuck 125g of the chopped chocolate between the croissant slices.

2 Making the chocolate custard

Place sugar, eggs and vanilla in a large bowl and whisk until combined. Place cream, milk and remaining 50g chocolate in a saucepan and stir over low heat until chocolate melts. Remove from heat and slowly whisk chocolate mixture into the egg mixture until combined. Transfer to a jug, then pour custard over croissant mixture in ramekins. Sprinkle with chopped macadamias, then stand for 5 minutes for the custard to soak into the croissants.

3 Cooking the puddings

Place ramekins on an oven tray and bake for 25 minutes or until set and golden on top. To serve, dust puddings with icing sugar and top with a dollop of double cream.

MIX IT UP
For jaffa-flavoured puddings, add the finely grated zest of 1 orange to the custard. You could also substitute slivered almonds or chopped pecans for the macadamias.

MY SCORE /10

MY SCORE   /10

Hokey pokey cheesecakes

SERVES: 6
PREPARATION: 20 MINS
Allow an extra 3 hours for cheesecakes to set.

150g butternut snap biscuits
60g unsalted butter, melted

Filling
150g jersey caramels
375g cream cheese, softened
180ml (¾ cup) sweetened condensed milk
2 x 50g Violet Crumble bars, chopped

1 Preparing the muffin pan
Grease 6 holes of a 180ml (¾-cup) Texas muffin pan. Cut 12 x 3cm-wide strips of baking paper long enough to extend beyond the rim of the holes, then place 2 in each hole to form a cross (these will be used as handles to lift the cheesecakes out).

2 Making the base
Process biscuits in a food processor to fine crumbs. Add butter and process to combine. Divide biscuit mixture among the muffin holes and, using the bottom of a small glass, press down firmly to compact.

3 Making the filling
Place caramels in a heatproof bowl. Place bowl over a small saucepan of simmering water and stir until melted. Using an electric mixer, beat cream cheese and condensed milk until smooth and combined. Using a large spoon, gently fold in Violet Crumble, then the caramel, to create a swirled effect. Divide the mixture among the prepared muffin holes, then lift the pan and tap it gently on the benchtop to remove any air pockets. Refrigerate for 3 hours or until firm.

4 Serving the cheesecakes
To serve, using the paper as handles, carefully lift cheesecakes from the muffin holes and transfer to a platter.

The inspiration for these vanilla and toffee cheesecakes comes from everyone's favourite ice-cream flavour, hokey pokey!

ABOUT JADE

Ten-year-old Jade comes from Queensland and, among her specialties, which include Asian dishes and roasts, she loves to bake. Like so many of the Junior MasterChefs, her favourite hobby is... cooking! She also enjoys watching cooking shows on TV and just reading recipes for fun.

Jade
White chocolate sticky date puddings with white chocolate and raspberry sauces

SERVES: 10
PREPARATION: 25 MINS
COOKING: 20 MINS

140g (1 cup) dried pitted dates, roughly chopped
½ tsp bicarbonate of soda
100g unsalted butter, softened, plus extra melted, to brush
75g (⅓ cup) caster sugar
1 egg
75g (½ cup) self-raising flour, sifted, plus extra, to dust
100g white chocolate, roughly chopped
Icing sugar and mint leaves, to serve

White chocolate sauce
250ml (1 cup) pouring cream
175g white chocolate, roughly chopped
½ tsp vanilla extract

Raspberry sauce
½ tsp cornflour
2 tbs caster sugar
250g raspberries, plus extra, to serve

1 Preheat oven to 180C. Brush 10 holes of a 12-hole (80ml/⅓-cup) muffin pan with butter. Dust with flour.

2 Combine dates and 125ml (½ cup) water in a saucepan and bring to the boil. Remove from heat and stir in bicarbonate of soda. Cool.

3 Using an electric mixer, beat butter and sugar until pale. Add egg and beat well. Stir in date mixture, flour and chocolate. Spoon batter into muffin holes and smooth tops. Bake for 15 minutes. Cool for 10 minutes in pan, then turn out onto a wire rack to cool.

4 Meanwhile, to make white chocolate sauce, place cream in a saucepan. Bring almost to the boil over medium heat. Place chocolate in a heatproof bowl, add cream and stir to combine. Cover with plastic wrap and stand for 3 minutes or until chocolate melts. Stir in vanilla until combined. Makes 1½ cups.

5 To make raspberry sauce, combine all ingredients with 60ml (¼ cup) water in a saucepan and bring to the boil over high heat. Reduce heat to medium and simmer, stirring occasionally, for 10 minutes or until thickened. Strain through a fine sieve into a bowl. Makes ¾ cup. Dust puddings with icing sugar and serve with extra raspberries, sauces and mint leaves.

This looks spectacular. You took something basic to another level!
GEORGE CALOMBARIS

MY SCORE   /10

To say this dish is amazing
is an understatement.
ANNA GARE

MY SCORE   /10

Lily
Passionfruit pavlova roulade

SERVES: 6
PREPARATION: 40 MINS
COOKING: 15 MINS
Allow 1½ hrs for the meringue to cool and set.

4 egg whites, at room
   temperature
1 tsp white vinegar
150g (⅔ cup) caster
   sugar, plus 2 tsp extra
1 tsp vanilla extract
1 tsp cornflour
¼ cup very finely
   chopped nuts
   (macadamias,
   pecans or almonds)
¼ tsp ground cinnamon
125g each raspberries
   and blueberries

Passionfruit filling
8 passionfruit
180ml (¾ cup) thickened
   cream
½ tsp vanilla extract

1 Preheat oven to 180C. Grease a 26cm x 32cm Swiss roll pan, then line with baking paper.

2 Using an electric mixer, whisk egg whites and vinegar until soft peaks form (see Lesson #4, page 29). Gradually add sugar, 1 tablespoon at a time, beating well after each addition, until mixture is thick and glossy. Add vanilla and cornflour, and whisk briefly to combine.

3 Working quickly, spread mixture evenly into prepared pan. Combine nuts, extra 2 tsp sugar and cinnamon and sprinkle evenly over meringue. Bake for 12 minutes or until meringue springs back when gently pressed. (Get an adult to help you with the next step.) When cooked, remove from oven, place a clean tea towel over top, then a chopping board, and invert together. Carefully lift away pan, then gently peel back baking paper. Cover with plastic wrap. Cool for 30 minutes.

4 Meanwhile, to make passionfruit filling, cut 2 passionfruit in half and scoop out pulp. Reserve pulp (with seeds) to serve. Repeat with remaining 6 passionfruit, then process pulp briefly in a food processor. Strain through a fine sieve into a jug. Discard seeds. Using an electric mixer, whisk cream, 60ml (¼ cup) passionfruit juice and vanilla to firm peaks (do not over-beat).

ABOUT LILY

Lily is 10 years old and comes from New South Wales. Her greatest inspiration is her grandma (though Adriano Zumbo comes close!). This big-hearted girl raised hundreds of dollars for the Queensland Flood Appeal by setting up a temporary cafe in her street. We'd certainly pay big bucks for this fab pav, which helped win her the egg mystery box challenge.

5 Remove plastic wrap and spread passionfruit filling over cooled pavlova, leaving a 2cm border at the short end furthest from you. Roll up from the other short end by lifting the tea towel to ease meringue into a roll, using the towel as a guide. Transfer to a platter (still rolled in tea towel), then refrigerate for 1 hour or until ready to serve. To serve, remove tea towel and cut roulade into thick slices. Drizzle with remaining passionfruit juice and reserved passionfruit pulp and scatter over berries.

Caroline
Apple rhubarb crumble with custard

ABOUT CAROLINE

Eleven-year-old Caroline comes from New South Wales and loves cooking different cuisines, especially Chinese inspired by her dad. She considers her style simple, but likes to put her own twist on classics – this time-honoured dessert charmed both Anna Gare and Matt Moran in the very first heat of the competition.

SERVES: 8
PREPARATION: 15 MINS
COOKING: 30 MINS

60ml (¼ cup) orange juice
1.2kg pink lady apples
75g (⅓ cup) caster sugar, plus 2 tsp extra
1 bunch rhubarb, trimmed, cut into 2cm lengths
1 tsp ground cinnamon

Crumble
110g (¾ cup) plain flour
45g (½ cup) oats
200g (1 cup firmly packed) brown sugar
125g cold unsalted butter, chopped

Custard
430ml (1¾ cups) pouring cream
1 tsp vanilla extract
4 egg yolks
110g (½ cup) caster sugar

1 Preheat oven to 180C. Grease 8 x 375ml (1½-cup) ramekins. Place orange juice in a large bowl. Peel, core and cut apples into 2cm pieces, adding to juice as you go. Toss well.

2 Place 500ml (2 cups) water and 75g sugar in a saucepan, bring to the boil over medium heat, stirring to dissolve sugar. Add rhubarb and apple mixture to pan and reduce heat to medium. Cook for 3 minutes or until fruit is slightly soft. Using a slotted spoon, divide fruit among ramekins. Discard liquid. Sprinkle cinnamon and extra sugar over fruit.

3 To make crumble, combine flour, oats and sugar in a large bowl. Using fingertips, rub in butter until mixture resembles coarse breadcrumbs. Divide mixture among ramekins. Place ramekins on an oven tray and bake for 25 minutes or until crumble is golden.

4 Meanwhile, to make custard, place cream and vanilla in a saucepan and bring almost to the boil over medium heat. Set aside for 7 minutes or until slightly cooled. Whisk yolks and sugar in a large heatproof bowl until thick and pale. Slowly whisk warm cream into egg mixture. Place bowl over a saucepan of simmering water. Using a wooden spoon, stir mixture continuously for 12 minutes or until custard thickens. Do not allow mixture to get too hot. Strain into a jug. Serve custard with crumbles.

I love that combination of
apple and rhubarb – I'm going
to have another spoonful!
MATT MORAN
MY SCORE   /10

MY SCORE   /10

Golden syrup dumplings

SERVES: 4
PREPARATION: 10 MINS
COOKING: 10 MINS

185g (1¼ cups)
  self-raising flour
50g unsalted butter,
  chopped
1 egg, lightly beaten
2 tbs milk
25g (⅓ cup) flaked
  almonds, roasted
Vanilla ice-cream, to serve

Syrup
330g (1½ cups)
  caster sugar
60g unsalted butter
1 cinnamon quill
90g (¼ cup) golden syrup
  (see Chef's Tip)

Golden syrup is made from sugar cane, and was invented in 1883 in Scotland. It is still sold in the same tins that were designed in 1885!

1 Making the dumplings
Place flour and butter in a large bowl. Using your fingertips, rub butter into flour until the mixture resembles breadcrumbs. Make a well in the centre, add egg and milk, then stir until a soft dough forms. Roll tablespoonfuls of dough into 12 balls.

2 Making the syrup
To make syrup, place sugar, butter, cinnamon, golden syrup and 500ml (2 cups) water in a large saucepan, then stir over low heat until combined. Bring syrup to a simmer over medium heat.

3 Cooking the dumplings
Using a slotted spoon, carefully lower the dumplings into the syrup. Cover with a lid and cook for 8 minutes or until dumplings are puffed and springy to the touch. Discard cinnamon quill, then divide dumplings among bowls, spoon over the syrup and sprinkle with roasted almonds. Serve dumplings immediately with vanilla ice-cream.

Chef's Tip
To measure golden syrup easily, lightly oil your measuring cup or spoon first – that way, the syrup won't stick and you'll have a more accurate measurement.

Chocolate fondants

SERVES: 4
PREPARATION: 20 MINS
COOKING TIME: 15 MINS

250g dark chocolate
   (70% cocoa
   solids), chopped
40g butter
3 eggs, lightly beaten
110g (½ cup)
   caster sugar
50g (⅓ cup) plain
   flour, sifted
Dutch cocoa (see Chef's
   Tip, page 37), to dust
Crème fraîche (see
   Chef's Tip), to serve

1 Making the chocolate mixture
Preheat oven to 200C. Lightly grease 4 x 180ml (¾-cup) metal dariole moulds, then line the base of each mould with a round of baking paper. Fill a small saucepan one-third full with water and bring to a simmer. Place chocolate and butter in a heatproof bowl, then place the bowl over the saucepan (don't allow the bowl to touch the water – see Lesson #15, page 103). Stir chocolate mixture until melted and combined. Set aside.

2 Making the batter
Using an electric mixer, whisk eggs and sugar on high speed for 5 minutes or until thick and pale. Using a metal spoon, fold in flour until combined, then fold cooled chocolate mixture into the egg mixture until combined.

3 Cooking the fondants
Divide batter among moulds, then place on an oven tray. Bake for 12 minutes or until the tops of the fondants are just firm to the touch (the centres should remain a little undercooked). Using oven gloves, remove fondants from the oven. Carefully run a small knife around the edge of the moulds to loosen (get an adult to help you as the moulds will be hot). Invert fondants onto plates and peel away baking paper. Dust with cocoa and serve immediately with crème fraîche.

Chef's Tip
Crème fraîche is a French lightly soured cream. It is available, from selected supermarkets and delis. Substitute regular light sour cream.

TOP TIP
The fondant batter can be made up to 6 hours ahead, placed in the moulds and stored, covered, in the fridge. To bake, allow an extra 3 minutes' cooking time.

Fondant means 'melting' in French, and this is exactly how the centre of your chocolate fondants should turn out – meltingly soft and gooey!

MY SCORE   /10

CoOking NOtes

Adult supervision It is important to ensure you have adult supervision as you cook, especially when it involves using sharp knives, cooking with hot oil and taking items out of the oven.

Baking All oven temperatures are for conventional, non-fan-forced ovens.

Chocolate Cocoa solids give chocolate its flavour. Dark chocolate has a higher percentage of cocoa solids than milk chocolate. Choose from 55% to 85%, depending on how bitter you like it. Avoid chocolate with added butter or oil, as it's not suitable for cooking.

Cream We've used three main types in our recipes: pouring cream (35% butter fat) is also labelled as pure cream; thickened cream (35% butter fat) contains gelatine and is most suitable for whipping; double cream (48% butter fat or more) is usually for serving.

Eggs We recommend using eggs laid by free-range poultry. Use eggs at room temperature. Unless specified, all eggs used are 59g (extra large).

Grinding & crushing If you don't have a mortar and pestle, use the small bowl of a food processor. Or seal spices in a plastic bag and bash them with a rolling pin or the flat side of a meat mallet.

Hygiene Always wash your hands with soap and warm water before you start cooking and don't dry wet or sticky hands on your clothes – use a clean tea towel or paper towel. Always scrub your nails before and after cooking. Before you start, remove any jewellery. It's a good idea to tie your hair back, too. No one likes to find a runaway hair in their dinner! And finally, wear an apron (or clothes you don't mind getting dirty!) to ensure you don't stain your clothes.

Lemon juice When the flesh of some fruit, such as apples, pears and bananas, is exposed to air, it oxidises, resulting in discolouration. This can be slowed by tossing them in lemon juice.

Onions We've used these varieties: onions refer to the brown variety; red onions are also called Spanish onions; spring onions are the long, thin green variety; eschalots are the small, sweet variety with golden-coloured skin; Asian red eschalots are the small sweet variety with pinky-red skin, available from Asian grocers.

Seasoning Unless stated otherwise, 'season' means to season with salt and pepper.

Weights & sizes For accuracy, it's better to weigh ingredients rather than use cup measurements. Fruit and vegetables are medium-sized unless specified.

iNdex

MasterChef MAGAZINE

Editor-in-Chief Trudi Jenkins
Managing Editor Sally Feldman
Food Director Sophia Young
Creative Director Scott Cassidy
Project Art Directors Anita Jokovich, Jacqui Porter
Project Sub-editor Robin Hill
Photographer Jeremy Simons
Series Photographers Stuart Bryce
Nigel Wright
Stylist Michelle Noerianto
Project Food Editor Rebecca Truda
Project Food Preparation Lucy Busuttil
Recipe Testing Nick Banbury, Dominic Smith
Bronwen Warden

Production Director Mark Moes
Production Manager Leanne George
Editorial Coordinator Alice Lindley
Editorial enquiries (02) 8062 2791,
masterchef@newsmagazines.com.au
Group Publisher, Food Fiona Nilsson
Chief Executive Officer Sandra Hook

Contributors George Calombaris, Anna Gare, Gary Mehigan, Neil Perry, Matt Moran, Kumar Mahadevan, Luke Nguyen, Alessandro Pavoni

Thanks
top3 by design (top3.com.au)

Enquiries: Locked Bag 5030, Alexandria, NSW 2015, tel: (02) 8062 2791, email: masterchef@newsmagazines.com.au. Melbourne Office, HWT Tower, Level 5, 40 City Rd, Southbank, Vic 3006, tel: (03) 9292 2000, fax: (03) 9292 1695. *MasterChef Magazine* is published by News Magazines Pty Ltd (ACN 088 923 906), 170–180 Bourke Rd, Alexandria, NSW 2015, tel: (02) 8062 2666, fax: (02) 8062 2166. News Magazines Pty Ltd is a wholly owned subsidiary of News Limited (ACN 007 871 178). Copyright 2011 by News Magazines Pty Ltd. All rights reserved. MasterChef © 2011 Shine (Aust) Pty Ltd. Junior MasterChef is a trademark of Shine (Aust) Pty Ltd. Licensed by Shine 360°. All rights reserved. Junior MasterChef™ produced by Shine Australia for the Ten Network based on a format by Franc Roddam. Colour separations Sinnott Bros. Printed by Offset Alpine, 42 Boorea Street, Lidcombe NSW 2141, under ISO14001 Environmental Certification. Paper fibre is from certified forests and audited sources. Distributed by Gordon and Gotch Australia Pty Ltd, tel: 1300 650 666. No material may be reproduced without prior written permission of the publisher.